GETTING TO KNOW THE BIBLE

Getting to Know

THE BIBLE

By

REV. JOSEPH F. X. CEVETELLO

SOCIETY OF ST. PAUL
CANFIELD - NEW YORK - DERBY - DETROIT

IMPRIMI POTEST:

Victor Viberti, S.S.P.

Staten Island, Sept. 15, 1957 **Censor Del.**

NIHIL OBSTAT:

Rt. Rev. Msgr. Joseph H. Brady, S.T.D.
Censor Librorum

IMPRIMATUR:

† Most Reverend Thomas A. Boland, S.T.D.

Newark, N. J., April 12, 1956 **Archbishop of Newark**

Library of Congress catalog card number: 57-12244

To

My Queen and Mother in Heaven

And

My Mother on Earth

PREFACE

THE distinction between reading and study is altogether valid as such, but one which has no particular relevance in some cases. The Bible is such a case. A person cannot truly read the Bible without study. Bible reading is necessarily study-reading. The reasons for this rise up upon a moment's reflection. The Bible is an old book, first written in the strange tongues, Hebrew, Aramaic, and Greek, in an ancient culture and a distant land.

The Scriptures were completed almost two thousand years ago and were begun about a thousand years before that. Consider the obvious fact that any book must be read against the context of its times and the ordinary situation that most readers are little informed on those times, and the need of some study appears as inescapable logic. Unawareness of these fundamental facts leads to haphazard and in some cases mischievous use of the Bible.

In this little book Father Cevetello, a former student of mine, has endeavored to fill the need of study for college students and interested laymen. He does not pretend to be a professional biblical scholar, but he has taught the Bible to college students for some years with interest and zeal. He is aware of their needs. I believe this book will be an answer to their need and to that of many others who love the Bible. I heartily recommend it as such, and ask God to give it abundant blessings.

Darlington, N. J.

VERY REV. MSGR. JOHN J. DOUGHERTY

CONTENTS

PART THREE — *THE NEW TESTAMENT*

INTRODUCTION

IT is not with little trepidation that the writer begins this book dealing with the greatest of all books and the most popular "Best Seller," the Bible. He is fully aware of his limitations, realizing that there are many scholars much more qualified than he. It is for this reason, and others, that he wishes to declare in the very beginning of this work that he makes no pretense of offering to the public a thoroughly scholarly and scientific work. However, in all fairness to the reader, the author assures him that what is in this book has been chosen judiciously from the many books written by Scripture scholars, past and present, so that the reader might be presented with the latest available data on the Scriptures.

The need for a popular treatment (insofar as this is possible), a sort of introduction to the Bible, was brought to the attention of the writer while he labored as assistant pastor in a busy parish and instructor in Religion at Seton Hall University. Aware of the Church's desire that her children read the Bible and aware also that the Bible is not the easiest of the books to read and understand, the author feels that a simple work should be presented to the public which would provide a knowledge of the general construction of the Bible and of some specific considerations and difficulties of the Old and New Testament. It is for this reason that he writes this book, mindful at all times of his limitations, yet desirous that the contents of the holiest of all books be more understandable to the average Catholic reader.

* * *

The book is divided into three sections. *The first section* considers the Bible in general, treating briefly of its general construction, its inspiration, the number of its books, its languages and manuscripts, etc.

The second section, dealing with the Old Testament, after briefly considering the history of the Jewish people, the geography of the Holy Land, and some particular considerations and problems of the Old Testament—this for the sake of giving the reader a general background—considers each book of the Old Testament, dwelling briefly, where possible, on the author, time and place of composition, content outline, and some particular considerations.

The third section, on the New Testament, follows very closely the form of the second section. However, two chapters (XIII and XIV) are given to the early, hidden, and public life of Our Blessed Savior and to His Passion, Death, and Resurrection. Of necessity these chapters are sketchy. Chapter XV, after a brief introduction on miracles and parables in general, gives in outline form the miracles and parables of Christ, together with the identification of the places where they occurred and the passages in the Gospels where the accounts will be found.

The appendixes contain material which might prove useful to the general reader of the Bible, as well as to the instructor in Religion, or to the priest in his capacity as preacher and teacher.

The writer wishes to thank most sincerely the Very Reverend Monsignor John J. Dougherty, S.Scr.D., for his invaluable help and for his writing the Preface to this book. The author is most grateful to the typists, Anne Caltagirone, Josephine G. Petronaci, and Augustus J. Bevilacqua, to the publishers who have generously granted permission for the use of passages from their books, and to anyone who has cooperated in any way in the production of this work.

Old Testament texts have been taken from the Douay Version and the Confraternity Edition; New Testament Texts have been taken from the Confraternity Edition of the New Testament. The author is grateful to the publishers for the permission given to use these texts.

All statements herein are unreservedly submitted to the judgment of the Holy See.

If the reader of this simple work is encouraged to read and love the Sacred Scriptures, then the author asks a brief prayer in return.

Montclair, New Jersey

REV. JOSEPH F. X. CEVETELLO

PART I

THE BIBLE IN GENERAL

CHAPTER I

WHAT IS THE BIBLE?

THE BIBLE is "the accepted collection of sacred books which were composed under the positive influence of the Holy Spirit, were written at various times and in various places by men whom God had chosen for this purpose, and were received by the Church as inspired."[1]

Word of God. God is the Primary Author of the Bible; men are the secondary authors of the Bible. Since God is the Author, we rightly call the Bible the Word of God. Hence, the Bible is considered a sacred book and free from error. (Cf. Chapter II).

Word "Bible." The word "Bible" comes from the Greek *Ta Biblia,* a plural meaning "the little books." Actually, the Bible is a collection of seventy-two (some say seventy-three) books; hence, it really is a library of inspired books.

Other Names for the Bible. Other names given to the Bible are: the Scriptures, Holy Scripture, Scripture, Sacred Books, Testament, Inspired Writings, Word of God.

Main Division of the Bible

The Bible is divided into two main sections called the Old Testament and the New Testament. (When referring to either testament, we will use the abbreviations O. T. for the former and N. T. for the latter).

The word "testament," in this connection, does not have the usual present-day meaning (e.g., a will); it is from the Latin and refers to a fundamental idea of Revelation, that of covenant, agreement, or compact between God and man.

The *OLD TESTAMENT* consists of those books which contain God's Revelation to the Jews before the coming of Christ and which were written before His time. The O. T. books are grouped into the following categories:

1. HISTORICAL BOOKS, which concern the creation of the world, history of the Jews, etc.
2. DIDACTIC OR SAPIENTIAL OR MORAL BOOKS, which instruct us about heavenly wisdom and morality.
3. PROPHETIC BOOKS, which contain God's message to men and predictions of the future.

The *NEW TESTAMENT* consists of those books which contain God's Revelation since the coming of Christ and which were written after Christ. The N. T. books may be grouped into the following categories:

1. HISTORICAL BOOKS, which contain the life and works of Christ and the history of the early Church.
2. DIDACTIC BOOKS, which are the epistles or letters of the Apostles containing instructions, exhortations, etc., to individuals or groups of Christians.
3. PROPHETIC BOOK, The Apocalypse of St. John.

Number of Books in the Bible

Catholics, in accordance with the computation of the Council of Trent (Sess. IV) recognize forty-five books in the O. T., and twenty-seven in the N. T. Some Catholics, by counting Jeremias and Baruch as separate books, arrive at a total of forty-six in the O. T.

The JEWS accept only thirty-nine books in the O. T., and originally they even reduced this number by an artificial division to twenty-four or twenty-two, on the basis of the number of letters in the Hebrew alphabet.

The PROTESTANTS follow the Jewish tradition of thirty-nine books in the O. T., but agree with Catholics in recognizing twenty-seven books in the N. T. (Cf. Chapter III).

The Books of the Bible

The abbreviations given for the books of the Bible are taken from the Confraternity edition of the Bible. These abbreviations will be used throughout this book.

THE OLD TESTAMENT BOOKS:

Historical Books:

Genesis	(Gn)	4 Kings	(4Kgs)
Exodus	(Ex)	1 Paralipomenon	(1 Par)
Leviticus	(Lv)	(Chronicles)	
Numbers	(Nm)	2 Paralipomenon	(2 Par)
Deuteronomy	(Dt)	(Chronicles)	
Josue	(Jos)	Esdras	(Esd)
Judges	(Jgs)	Nehemias (2 Esdras)	(Neh)
Ruth	(Ru)	Tobias	(Tb)
1 Samuel (Kings)	(1Sm)	Judith	(Jdt)
2 Samuel (Kings)	(2Sm)	Esther	(Est)
3 Kings	(3Kgs)	1 Machabees	(1Mc)
		2 Machabees	(2Mc)

Didactic Books:

Job	(Jb)	Ezechiel	(Ez)
Psalms	(Ps)	Daniel	(Dn)
Proverbs	(Prv)	Osee	(Os)
Ecclesiastes	(Eccl)	Joel	(Jl)
Canticle of Canticles	(Ct)	Amos	(Am)
Wisdom	(Wis)	Abdias	(Abd)
Sirach (Ecclesiasticus)	(Sir)	Jonas	(Jon)
		Micheas	(Mi)
		Nahum	(Na)

Prophetic Books:

		Habacuc	(Hb)
Isaias	(Is)	Sophonias	(So)
Jeremias	(Jer)	Aggeus	(Ag)
Lamentations	(Lam)	Zacharias	(Za)
Baruch	(Bar)	Malachias	(Mal)

The New Testament Books:

Historical Books:

		1 Thessalonians	(1 Thes)
Gospel of St. Matthew	(Mt)	2 Thessalonians	(2 Thes)
Gospel of St. Mark	(Mk)	1 Timothy	(1 Tm)
Gospel of St. Luke	(Lk)	2 Timothy	(2 Tm)
Gospel of St. John	(Jn)	Titus	(Ti)
Acts of the Apostles	(Act)	Philemon	(Phlm)
		Hebrews	(Heb)

Didactic Books:

		St. James	(Jas)
		1 St. Peter	(1 Pt)
Romans	(Rom)	2 St. Peter	(2 Pt)
1 Corinthians	(1 Cor)	1 St. John	(1 Jn)
2 Corinthians	(2 Cor)	2 St. John	(2 Jn)
Galatians	(Gal)	3 St. John	(3 Jn)
Ephesians	(Eph)	St. Jude	(Jude)
Philippians	(Phil)		
Collossians	(Col)		

Prophetic Book:

Apocalypse of St. John (Ap)

CHAPTERS AND VERSES. The Cardinal Archbishop of Canterbury, Stephen Langton, first divided the Bible into chapters of approximately equal length about 1226.

The division of the chapters into verses received its final form from the printer Robert Estienne in 1551.

Interpretation and Reading of the Bible

INTERPRETATION OF THE BIBLE. Only the Catholic Church, which is Christ's Church and the custodian of Revelation, can adequately and properly interpret the Holy Scriptures.

Unlike Protestant sects, the Catholic Church forbids private interpretation of the Bible because the average person is not qualified and properly equipped to interpret the Word of God. Only the Church can do so with authority.

The Vatican Council renewed the Trent's Decree on the Interpretation of Holy Scripture in the following terms:

"We, renewing the said decree, declare this to be its meaning: that in matters of faith and morals pertaining to the building up of Christian Doctrine, that is to be held as the true sense of Sacred Scripture which Holy Mother Church hath held and doth hold, to whom it belongeth to judge of the true sense and interpretation of the Holy Scriptures, and therefore that it is permitted to no one to interpret the said Scriptures against this sense, or likewise, against the unanimous consent of the Fathers."[2]

MAY CATHOLICS READ THE BIBLE? Yes. Not only may they read the Bible, but in order to encourage them, the

Church grants to Catholics who read the Bible for at least a quarter of an hour "with the great reverence due to the Divine Word and after the manner of spiritual reading an indulgence of three years." (S. C. Ind. Dec. 13, 1898; S. P. Ap. March 22, 1932).

If this be so, why did the Church chain the Bibles in the Middle Ages?

They were chained, not to keep the people from reading them (they still could be read in the Churches even though they were chained), but to keep the people from taking them out of the Churches. We must remember that Bibles were scarce and expensive in those days because they had to be made by hand.

CHAPTER II

THE BIBLE IS DIVINELY INSPIRED

Meaning of Inspiration

POPE LEO XIII, in his Encyclical "Providentissimus Deus," describes inspiration as "a supernatural impulse by which the Holy Ghost urged and moved the sacred writers to write and assisted them while they wrote in such a way that they understood exactly, willed to report faithfully, and expressed with infallible truth all that God ordered, and only what He ordered them to write."

Another definition: "Inspiration, by which God is truly the principal author of the sacred book while man is the secondary author, consists in this, that in the production of the sacred book God uses man as an instrument elevated by supernatural power."[3]

Some Observations on Inspiration

1. "The divine power acts on the intellect of the sacred writer. At the outset, it makes him perceive ideas and facts more clearly. If these ideas or facts are absolutely unknown to him, the sacred writer must first of all receive a revelation in the strict sense. But if these ideas or facts are known to him, or if he can obtain a knowledge of them through his

own efforts,—investigation of documents, interrogation of witnesses—God gives him no information; He lets him work like any other conscientious writer, but He gives him supernatural assistance. Therefore, the use of written sources and of oral witnesses is perfectly compatible with scriptural inspiration."[4]

2. Inspiration acts not only on the intellect, but also on the will of the sacred writer. "The sacred writer will look for written documents, will question witnesses, and will make all the effort necessary for the accomplishment of his task. In all this, God impels him and sustains him until the work is completed. The sacred writer undergoes this divine impulse without necessarily being conscious of it; he undergoes it infallibly, without his liberty being suppressed or even merely diminished."

3. "This divine influence, which acts by way of scriptural inspiration on the will of the sacred writer, does not exclude outside factors which also may have acted on him, and with which we are familiar. Thus we know that Saint Mark and Saint John wrote their Gospels at the demand of the faithful in Rome and in Asia."

4. "The sacred writer receives special assistance while he is writing his book. It matters little whether he writes it himself or, according to the custom of the ancients, dictates it to a secretary."[5]

What Inspiration Does Not Mean

For the proper understanding of inspiration, the following must be kept in mind:

1. For a book to be inspired, it is not necessary that its author be known.

2. "It is not necessary, in order that a book should be inspired, that it should be officially recognized as such. Inspiration comes from God; canonicity, that is to say, inclusion in the list of Holy Scriptures, (Cf. Chapter III) is the result of the decision made by the Church."[6]

Proof of Inspiration of the Bible

INTERNAL PROOF. For Scriptural proof of the inspiration of the *OLD TESTAMENT* we might offer the following passages from the O. T. and the N. T.:

ISAIAS 8:1—"The Lord said to me: 'Take thee a great book, and write in it with a man's pen.'"

JEREMIAS 30:2—"Write all the words I have spoken to thee in a book."

Other O. T. passages: Ex 34:27; Dt 31:19; Jer 36:1-3, 9:2; Ps 1:2; Jos 1:8; 2 Sm 23:2. These texts show the moral influence of God on the production of the books.

MATTHEW 22:43—"Jesus said to them: 'How then does David in the Spirit call him Lord?'" This text shows the immediate influence of the Spirit on David.

2 TIMOTHY 3:15f.—"For from thy infancy thou hast known the Sacred Writings, which are able to instruct thee unto salvation by the faith which is in Christ Jesus. All Scripture is inspired by God and useful for teaching, for reproving, for correcting, for instructing in justice; that the man of God may be perfect, equipped for every good work." This text directly affirms the inspiration of Scripture.

For the internal proof of the *NEW TESTAMENT* we might consider the following:

> 2 PETER 3:15-16—"Just as our dear brother Paul also, according to the wisdom given him, has written to you as indeed he did in all his epistles, speaking in them of these things. In these epistles there are certain things difficult to understand, which the unlearned and unstable distort, just as they do to the rest of the Scriptures also, to their own destruction." St. Peter places St. Paul's writings in the same category as "the other Scriptures," i. e. the O. T.

THE EARLY FATHERS AND EARLY WRITINGS considered the Bible divinely inspired. Among them were the following:

Justin (110-165)

Pseudo-Justin (c. 250)

Athenagoras (c. 177)

Theophilus of Antioch (c. 181)

Irenaeus (140-200)

Clement of Alexandria (150-211)

Origen (185-211)

THE POPES CONSIDERED THE BIBLE DIVINELY INSPIRED. Among the Popes the following made pronouncements concerning the divine inspiration of the Bible: Leo IX (1053), Innocent III (1208), Eugene IV (1441), Benedict XV (1920), Leo XIII (1893), Pius X (1907).

ECUMENICAL COUNCILS CONSIDERED THE BIBLE DIVINELY INSPIRED. *The Council of Trent* (1546) declares that she receives "all the books of both Testaments, both the Old and the New, since the one God is the Author of both."

Vatican Council (1869) "The Church holds those books as Sacred and Canonical not because, compiled by human industry alone, they were approved afterwards by their own authority; nor yet because they contain revelation without error; but because written under the inspiration of the Holy Spirit, they have God for their Author, and as such were handed down to the Church."

The Bible Is Free from Error

The original texts of the Bible are free from error. (This is called the "inerrancy" of the Bible). This has been the constant and universal teaching of the Church. God is the Author, the Inspirer of the Scriptures, and being God, He cannot teach error. He would be doing so, however, if in the Bible, which is His work, a single statement is found which is proven formally erroneous.

"Therefore, if one thinks that he perceives a contradiction between the different parts of the Bible or between the authentic statements of the Bible and any scientific truths whatsoever, this contradiction can be apparent only."[7]

"As Regards the Natural Sciences, it must be remembered that the Bible is essentially a religious book, and that it contains no specifically scientific teaching. To give us instruction of this kind, which would have been of no use for our salvation, the inspired authors would have needed a revelation in the strict sense, and this God did not grant them. Consequently, the Bible speaks of things in the realm of science according to appearances and not according to reality, adapting itself to popular language and the ideas of the time. In a given case, all that we can demand is that the language of the Bible should be in conformity with the appearances themselves. The Biblical Commission (June

30, 1909) has stated that the narrative of Creation is a popular account. In order to conform to the language of the time, the Bible speaks of the rising and setting of the sun, makes the moon the largest luminary after the sun, attributes the prolongation of daylight at the battle of Gabaon to the stopping of the sun, etc...

"But we must not conclude from the fact that the Bible contains no specifically scientific teaching that it contains no statements that concern science. On the contrary, the Bible states that the universe was created by God, that God intervened directly and specially at the time of the appearance of the first man and the first woman, it affirms the unity of the human species, etc...

"As REGARDS HISTORY, it must not be forgotten that, although the Bible contains no scientific teaching in the strict sense, it does contain, however, information and teaching which is truly historical. Furthermore, this historical content, which is easily understood by all, is often closely connected with dogma. This is the case in the O. T. in respect to the appearance of man, the unity of the human species, etc..."[8]

Protestant Attitude on Inspiration

Originally, the Protestant attitude on the inspiration of the Bible varied. Some held the traditional Catholic attitude, others merely looked on the Bible as another book, and others took the rigid and unreasonable view that even the commas, dashes, etc., of the Bible were inspired.

Protestants of today are divided on the idea of inspiration. Their opinions follow, to a great extent, the opinions of their forebears mentioned above.

CHAPTER III

THE BOOKS (CANON) OF THE BIBLE

CATHOLICS hold that there are seventy-two books in the Bible—forty-five in the O. T., and twenty-seven in the N. T. We shall demonstrate the fact that this number is not an arbitrary one. It is based on Scripture, Tradition, and the infallible teaching of the Church.

Definition of "Canon" and Other Terms

By the "CANON" of the Bible is meant that collection or list of books acknowledged and accepted by the Church as inspired.

The Greek word "Canon" means a rod or reed and so came to mean a measuring rod. The term came to be applied to those books which contained sound doctrine and which were thus regarded as the test or "measure" of such doctrine. From the very beginning of the Church, Scripture was regarded as a rule of faith and of life. Consequently, the word "Canon" of the Scriptures was used to designate that rule as written; the name "Canon" was thus given to the collection of inspired books.

The earliest certain evidence of this usage may be found in the works of St. Athanasius (c. 350) and probably even in the earliest works of Origen (254).

Canonical, the adjective, applied to a book included in the Canon of the Bible, has two sub-divisions:

PROTO-CANONICAL: "a book that was early included in the group and universally received without doubt."

DEUTERO-CANONICAL: "a book that was only later acknowledged by the universal Christian Church as belonging to the Canon or as being inspired." These books are:

Old Testament: Tobias, Judith, Baruch, Ecclesiasticus, Wisdom, 1 & 2 Machabees, certain additions to Esther and Daniel.

New Testament: Hebrews, James, 2 Peter, 2 & 3 John, Jude, and the Apocalypse.

(Note: A canonical book and an inspired book are concretely the same since all known inspired books are de facto in the Canon).

APOCRYPHAL BOOK: "a non-inspired book which by reason of its title or subject matter has some similarity to an inspired book."

PROTESTANT TERMINOLOGY REGARDING O. T. CANON. Their "canonical" books are our proto-canonical books. Their "apocryphal" books are our deutero-canonical books. Their "pseudopigraphal books" are the apocryphal books in our terminology.

Canon of the Old Testament

When we consult the sources to ascertain the Jewish Canon at the beginning of the Christian era, we discover two Canons in existence—one used by the Jews in Palestine and the other used by the Jews in Alexandria, Egypt.

PALESTINIAN JEWS recognized as belonging to the Canon of the O. T., those books which Catholics call "proto-canonical," i.e., those books of the O. T., which are not classified as deutero-canonical (cf. above). These Jews accepted twenty-two or twenty-four books—the former division making Ruth a part of Judges and Lamentations a part of Jeremias. These would be equivalent to all but seven in our O. T.

JOSEPHUS, Jewish historian, in his treatise "Against Apion," composed in 97-98, mentions twenty-two books.

THE FOURTH BOOK OF ESDRAS, composed about the end of the first century of our era, recognized the existence of an official collection of twenty-four books.

THE BABYLONIAN TALMUD (i.e., the written record of Jewish canon and civil law not contained in the first five books of the Bible), attributed to Juda the Holy (136-217), gives the list of twenty-four books which the Synagogue considered sacred and presents this list as one handed down by the Fathers.

THE NEW TESTAMENT contains either direct quotations, allusions, or reminiscences from nineteen of the O. T. books, i.e., the proto-canonical books.

ALEXANDRIAN JEWS recognized as belonging to the Canon of the O.T., all forty-five books which Catholics recognize, i.e., both proto-canonical and deutero-canonical books. These Jews used the Septuagint, i.e., a Greek translation of the O.T. which contained all forty-five books. (Cf. Chapter IV for the history of the Septuagint).

N.B. *Why the difference in number between the Palestinian and Septuagint versions?*:

1) Some scholars imagine that towards the end of the first century of our era, the Palestinian doctors removed from the canon several books which up to that time belonged to it.

2) Others have maintained that the Jews of Alexandria had a scriptural canon which was larger and richer than that of the Jews of Palestine. This may be due to the fact that the two groups did not have exactly the same ideas on questions of revelation and inspiration.

CHRISTIAN CANON OF THE OLD TESTAMENT. The Christian Canon of the O.T., contains all forty-five books of the Septuagint or the version used at Alexandria and other places outside of Palestine by Greek-speaking Jews.

It is generally agreed that Christ, and after Him, the Apostles, gave their sanction to the authority and the normative value of the books of the Palestinian canon (twenty-two or twenty-four books), for in their teaching, they frequently invoked the testimony of the Scriptures, which were regarded as the "Word of God."

However, have we the right to maintain that they also

guaranteed the canonicity of the other writings which the Alexandrian canon contained, i.e., the deutero-canonical books?

Since neither Christ nor the Apostles have given any formal pronouncement on the precise content of the Christian canon of the O. T., we must find the answer from examining the books of apostolic origin, and by tradition. In the N. T., there are references to several of the deutero-canonical books, especially from Ecclesiastes, Wisdom, and 2 Machabees.

"It is obvious that in practice, the Apostles and New Testament writers employed the Greek Bible without making any distinction between the books of the Jewish canon and the deutero-canonical books, except that they did not cite the latter as "Scripture." This procedure corresponded to that current among the Jews of Alexandria. It resulted in giving sanction to the authority of the deutero-canonical books, which were thus kept in the Scriptural collection of the early Church."[9]

Early Tradition: During the *first two centuries* the following Fathers of the Church acknowledged the deutero-canonical books—some Fathers mentioning some, others mentioning others; together they account for all:

ROME

Clement of Rome (d. 96 AD)
Hermas-book written (c. 140)
Hippolytus (c. 170-236)

FRANCE

Irenaeus (130-202)

WEST AFRICA

Tertullian (born 160)
Cyprian (190-258)

EAST

Polycarp (c. 115)
Didache (90-100)
Epistle of Barnabas (c. 100)
Athenagoras (c. 180)

The greater number of the Fathers of the 4th and 5th *centuries* considered the deutero-canonical books of the O. T. inspired:

GREEK FATHERS

Basil
Gregory of Nyssa
Didymus Caecus
John Chrysostom
Cyril of Alexandria

LATIN FATHERS

Lactantius

Ambrose
Orosius
Augustine
Leo the Great

SYRIAN FATHERS

Aphraates
Ephraem

Canon of the New Testament

"Just as the formation of the O.T. canon was a historical process, so also was that of the New Testament. There is this difference: whereas the process of the formation of O. T. covered centuries, the process of the N. T. formation was achieved in a much shorter period of time. The dates of composition of the N. T. books range from 40 to 100 A.D. The inspired books made their appearance during that time, but this does not say that immediately after appearance, they were universally recognized as inspired literature. The process of universal recognition or canonization was to take some centuries."[10]

The Bible of the early Christian Church was the O. T. But on a plane with the O. T., and if need be, above it, they placed the authority of "the Lord" or "the Gospel."

Early Proof of the New Testament Canon. If we demonstrate that the N. T. writings were considered inspired then we can conclude their canonicity, for canonical books are those accepted as inspired. That this is true first appears from the fact that the Christian writings are early placed in the same category as the O. T.

2 PETER 3:15-16: In this passage the writings of St. Paul are placed in the same category with the O. T.

LITURGICAL ASSEMBLIES: St. Justin (d. 165) explicitly refers to the custom of reading the Apostolic writings together with the O. T. readings.

Period 100 *to* 220 *A.D.* No catalog of the N. T. books was compiled during this time, but we have citations from the works of the Fathers of the time whereby we can build up the N. T. Canon. Some of the following Fathers mention all the books; others only some: together they account for the N. T. Canon.

Clement of Rome (Epistle to the Corinthians) (c. 96 A.D.)

Epistle of Barnabas (Pseudo-Barnabas, written between 100-150)

Polycarp (c. 110)

Didache (early writing) (90-100)

Hermas (c. 140)

Papias (c. 130)

Justin (c. 105-c. 165)

Iranaeus (135-203)

Tertullian (160-250)

Muratorian Fragment (c.180)

Clement of Alexandria (150-216)

Fathers of the third, fourth, and fifth centuries taken together account for the books of the N. T.

Ecclesiastical Documents Regarding Old Testament and New Testament Canons. The Fourth Council of Rome, c. 380 (Pope Damasus), The Council of Hippo, 393, The Third of Carthage, 397, The Fourth of Carthage, 419, and The Gelasian Decree (Pope Gelasius 494-496) mention the complete canon. The Ecumenical Council of Florence (1438-1445), in the Decree for the Jacobites, also professes the complete canons of the O. T. and N. T.

The Ecumenical Council of Trent (1545-1556), in the fourth session, April 8, 1546, infallibly defined, and hence made it an article of faith, the complete Canon of the N. T. and the O. T.

DECREE CONCERNING THE CANONICAL SCRIPTURES:

"The sacred and holy ecumenical and general synod of Trent lawfully assembled in the Holy Ghost ...following the examples of the orthodox Fathers, receives and venerates with an equal affection of piety and reverence, all the books, both of the Old and New Testament—seeing that one God is Author of both ...And it has thought it meet that a list of the sacred books be inserted in this decree, lest a doubt may arise in one's mind, which are the books that are received by this Synod... (Here the Council enumerates the seventy-two books that comprise the Canon of the Catholic Bible).(Cf. pp. 23ff.) But if anyone re· ceive not, as sacred and canonical, the said books entire with all their parts, as they have been usually read in the Catholic Church, and as they are contained in the old Latin vulgate edition; and knowingly and deliberately contemn the traditions aforesaid; let him be anathema."

Jewish and Protestant Views of Canon and of the Bible

The Jews, whom many Protestants follow, recognize only thirty-nine books of the O. T. They do not accept Tobias, Judith, Wisdom Sirach (Ecclesiasticus), Baruch, and 1 & 2 Machabees. Protestants are now in agreement with Catholics in counting twenty-seven books in the N. T., but this was not always so. "The first Protestant reformers did not agree on the extent of the Canon of the New Testament. Luther excluded the Apocalypse and the three Epistles—Hebrews, James, and Jude. Zwingli rejected the Apocalypse, and Oecolampadius eliminated all the deutero-canonical books... The Lutheran Chemnitz (d. 1588) excluded all the deutero-canonical books as being inferior, and this policy was followed by the Lutherans until the seventeenth century. Since, however, the Calvinists did not take any decisive stand against the seven deutero-canonical books, the Lutherans returned to the complete canon with this slight difference, that the four books rejected by Luther occupied the last position in printed editions of the Lutheran Bible."[11]

CHAPTER IV

LANGUAGES, TEXTS, VERSIONS OF THE BIBLE

Languages

THE languages in which the books of the Bible were originally written were Hebrew, Aramaic, and Greek.

HEBREW is a Semitic language (named from Sem, one of Noe's sons). Nearly all the books of the O. T. were written in Hebrew.

ARAMAIC is a branch of the Semitic. Christ spoke Aramaic while on earth. Portions of the book of Daniel (2:4-7, 28), and 1 Esdras (4:8-6, 18; 7:12-26), a verse in Jeremias (10:11), the last 6 chapters of Esther (10-16), all of Tobias and Judith, and the Gospel of St. Matthew (N. T.) were written in Aramaic.

GREEK, not the classical, but a dialect called "Koine" (common) was also used. In the O. T., Wisdom, 2 Machabees, and in the N. T., all but the Gospel of St. Matthew were written in this language.

How the Books Were Written

Papyrus was the ordinary material used for writing in Palestine in biblical times. Its rapid disintegration in damp climate explains why so few literary remains and biblical texts have been discovered in Palestine. Besides papyrus, leather or parchment was also used.

The form of the book in O. T. times was the roll or volume. A long strip of papyrus was attached at one end to a support around which it was rolled. The writing was usually only on the inner side of the papyrus and begun at the farther end so that the volume could be gradually unrolled as it was read. The book form was permitted later for private copies, but not for use in the synagogue.

The Septuagint

This is the Greek version of the O. T. containing all the forty-five canonical books (i.e., thirty-eight proto-canonical and seven deutero-canonical). It takes its name from the legend which says that at the request of Ptolemy II (285-240 B.C.) seventy or seventy-two scholars from Jerusalem translated at Alexandria, Egypt, in seventy-two days, all the canonical books of the O. T. It is now commonly recognized that it was begun about 250 B.C., and was completed about 100 B.C. It was used by the Apostles and early Christians.

The Vulgate

This is the most famous Latin translation of the Bible.

It is the work of St. Jerome (340-420) who undertook the translation at the request of Pope Damasus. St. Jerome worked from the "Old Latin" (Vetus Latina) text of the Bible, and from Hebrew, Aramaic, and Greek manuscripts. The Council of Trent declared the Vulgate to be the authentic (official) Latin version, and the one to be used publicly in the Western Church.

Oldest Manuscripts of the Bible

No "autographs" (originals) of the books of the Bible exist. This is due partly to the perishable material (papyrus) used by the writers, and partly to the fact that the Roman emperors (e.g. Edict of Diocletian, A.D. 303) decreed the destruction of the sacred books of the Christians.

Some of the very ancient copies of the Bible, called "Biblical manuscripts," which are still in existence are:

1. SINAITIC MANUSCRIPT: (fourth century), now in the British Museum.

2. VATICAN MANUSCRIPT: (fourth century), now in the Vatican Library.

3. ALEXANDRINE MANUSCRIPT: (fifth century), now in the British Museum.

4. PARISIAN OR EPHRAIM MANUSCRIPT: (fifth century).

NOTE: In October of 1948, the Wady Qumran Manuscripts (Dead Sea Scrolls) were found in a cave near Ain Feshkha, some eight miles from Jericho. The manuscripts date probably from 150 B.C., and contain the Book of Isaias and other books of the O. T.

Catholic English Versions

1. RHEIMS-DOUAY VERSION: translation from the Vulgate done by Catholic English scholars who were in exile in France. The English translation was made by Gregory Martin and the work was revised by William Allen and Richard Bristow. The N. T. was published at Rheims in 1582, and the O. T. at Douay in 1609-1610. Bishop Challoner (1749-1752) modernized the language of the text.

2. WESTMINSTER VERSION: N. T. made directly from the Greek in England (1914-1935), Fathers Lattey and Keating of the Society of Jesus being the general editors.

3. FR. SPENCER O.P. VERSION: N. T. done from the Greek in 1937 in the United States.

4. CONFRATERNITY EDITIONS: done in the U. S. by a group of scholars with the authorization of the Bishops of the United States. The N. T., translated from the Vulgate, was first published in 1941; the first eight books of the O. T. (from the original languages) in 1952.

5. THE RONALD KNOX TRANSLATION: (from the Vulgate) done in England. The N. T. was published in 1943; the first nineteen books of the O. T. in 1948; the remaining books of the O. T. in 1949-1950.[12]

Protestant English Versions

1. KING JAMES OR AUTHORIZED VERSION (AV): published in 1611 during the reign of King James I. This is not a new

translation, but a revision of an English Bible known as the Bishop's Bible (published in 1568). Anti-Catholic prejudice and modifications of words characterize this version. It is renowned for its excellent English style.

2. REVISED VERSION (RV) (1881-1885): is a modern critical revision done by English and American Protestant scholars at the insistence of the British Parliament.

3. AMERICAN STANDARD VERSION (SV): in 1901, the American group of the above committee brought out its own text of the Revised Version.

4. REVISED STANDARD VERSION (RSV): prepared by the Nationa lCouncil of the Church of Christ in the U.S.A. N. T. —1946; O. T.—1952.

First Printed Bible

The first Bible ever to be printed from movable type was made by Johann Gutenberg about 1452. This devout Franciscan tertiary chose the common Catholic version of the Bible, the text known as the Vulgate.

Abundance of Vernacular Bibles Before Wycliff

History attests that there were popular translations of the whole Bible and the Gospels in Spanish, Italian, Danish, French, Norwegian, Polish, Bohemian, and Hungarian for the Catholics of those lands before the days of printing.

It is a common fallacy that John Wycliffe was the first

to place an English translation of the Scriptures in the hands of the English people in 1382. "To begin with, we have a copy of the work of Caedmon, a monk of Whitby, in the end of the seventh century, consisting of great portions of the Bible in the common tongue. In the next century we have the well known translations of the Venerable Bede, a monk of Jarrow."[13] Each succeeding century saw more vernacular translations.

St. Thomas More, Lord Chancellor of England under King Henry VIII, has this to say in his "Dialogues III": "The whole Bible long before Wycliffe's day was by virtuous and well-learned men translated into the English tongue, and by good and godly people with devotion and soberness well and reverently read ... The clergy keep no Bibles from the laity but such translations as reproved for naught (i.e., bad) as was Wycliffe's."[14]

PART II

THE OLD TESTAMENT

CHAPTER V

HISTORY OF THE JEWS. GEOGRAPHY OF PALESTINE

History of the Jews

THE history of Israel begins with the call of Abraham to the worship of the one true God and the revelations made to him which foretold the destiny of his race.[1]

ABRAHAM left Haran in Mesopotamia with Lot at the divine command, receiving promises of special favors and of the Messianic blessings (covenant) (Gn 12). Abraham and Lot separated, Lot going to Sodom, Abraham to Mambra (Gn 13). God renewed the covenant (Gn 17). Sodom and Gomorrah were destroyed. Lot and his daughters escaped. His wife was destroyed for looking back on the doomed city (Gn 19).

ISAAC was born in the hundredth year of Abraham and the ninetieth of Sara (Gn 21). In his fortieth year, Isaac married his cousin Rebecca, and after twenty years of sterility, Rebecca conceived twins, Esau and Jacob, who became the fathers of rival nations (Gn 24-27).

JACOB's wives and their maidservants bore him eleven

sons (eleven of the twelve patriarchs of the tribes) and one daughter. His favorite son was Joseph. Joseph's brothers envied him, so they sold Joseph into slavery and told Jacob that a wild beast had devoured him (Gn 28-36).

JOSEPH was brought into Egypt where he eventually became very powerful. When famine struck the land of Jacob, Jacob sent his sons to procure grain. Joseph was then united with his family. Jacob and his family went to Egypt to live. This was the migration of the Israelites to Egypt—about 1700-1675 B.C.[2] (Gn 37-50).

MOSES was called by God to free the Jews who, for religious and political reasons, were being persecuted by the Egyptians. This was done after ten horrible plagues convinced the Pharaoh to let the Jews go. This departure—the Exodus—took place about 1300-1290 B.C. (Ex 1-14).

THE JEWS WANDERED IN THE DESERT for forty years, during which time they received many blessings from God as well as severe punishments for their transgressions. During this time the Ten Commandments were given to Moses on Mt. Sinai (Ex 15-18).

THE CONQUEST OF THE PROMISED LAND (Canaan) took place about 1250 under Josue. Canaan was partitioned among the tribes of Israel (Jos).

THE PERIOD OF JUDGES lasted from about 1225-1200 to about 1020 B.C. These Judges were: Othoniel, Aod, (Debbora and Barac), Gedeon, Thola, Jair, Jephte, Abesan, Ahialon, Abdon, Heli the high priest, Samson, and Samuel (Jgs).

THE PERIOD OF THE MONARCHY BEGAN WITH SAUL, the first king, who reigned from about 1020-1004 B.C. Saul lost favor with God when he disobeyed in offering sacrifice (1 Sm 9-31).

DAVID, succeeeding on the death of Saul, reigned from 1004-965 B.C. The twelve tribes of Israel were united under him. He captured Jerusalem from the Jebusites (about 998 B.C.), making it his capital. David's otherwise good life was marred by his sin of adultery with Bethsabee and his sending her husband to his death. God punished David severely for his transgressions; David repented. He is noted for the many beautiful psalms which he composed. He strengthened the spiritual, civil and military life of the Israelites. He died in the fortieth year of his reign, 965 B.C. (2 Sm & 1 Kgs).

SOLOMON succeeded his father, reigning from 965-926 B.C. He constructed the Temple at Jerusalem (961-955 B.C.). He was known for his wisdom and administrative ability. In his declining years his personal life degenerated and so did his kingdom. When he died in 926 B.C., his country was threatened with internal as well as external ruin (3 Kgs).

THE SCHISM began after Solomon's death, the kingdom splitting into two. The tribes of Juda and Benjamin under Roboam remained faithful to God and Solomon, becoming the Kingdom of Juda; the other ten tribes under Jeroboam became the Kingdom of Israel. From 926 until 882 B.C. hostilities existed between the groups; from 882 until 721 B.C. peace reigned. During this time the prophets (Amos, Osee, Isaias, Micheas) reminded the people of their duty to God (3Kgs).

THE CAPTIVITY OF THE JEWS began in 721 B.C. when the end of the northern Kingdom, Israel, came with the destruction of Samaria. In 587 B.C. the Kingdom of Juda was conquered by the Babylonians. Many were sent into exile, such prophets as Jeremias, Ezechiel, and Daniel going with them. In 539, Cyrus of Persia captured Babylon, freed the Jews, and permitted them to return to Jerusalem. In 333 B.C. Alexander the Great conquered the Persian Empire, and Israel came under Greek rule.

For many years the Israelites fought for their freedom, succeeded for a time in overcoming Syria, but ultimately came under the yoke of Rome. Herod the Great ruled them at the time of Christ's birth. (Cf. Appendix III.—*A Chronology of Hebrew History*).

Geography of Palestine

Palestine, the land of the Jews, is bounded on the north by the Lebanon and Anti-Lebanon mountains, on the east by the Syrian and Arabian deserts, on the south by the Syro-Egyptian desert, on the west by the Mediterranean Sea. These boundaries are natural, and put the land in quasi-isolation from its immediate neighbors.

The total area of Palestine is 15,600 square miles (about one third the size of New York). Its length is 150 miles, its width 125 miles.

A central range of mountains runs from Lebanon south through Palestine to the Sinai peninsula, looking very much like the country's spinal column. The mountains of Upper Galilee rise to over 3,000 feet while those of Lower Galilee go as high as 1,850 feet. Mount Tabor, the site of Christ's Transfiguration (Mt 17:1-9; Mk 9:1-9; Lk 9:28-36), rises solitary and majestic to a height of 1,843 feet, completely isolated from the surrounding hills. Some of the mountains of Judaea rise to over 2,000 feet. Jerusalem stands on two mountains of 2,400 and 2,450 feet.

The River Jordan, the most important of Palestine watercourses, traverses the whole length of the land. Most of its course runs several hundred feet below sea-level. Its swift current renders navigation impossible; hence trading on a wide scale is not possible.

The Lake of Galilee is a fresh water lake 12½ miles long, 7½ miles wide at its broadest and 126 feet at its greatest depth. Its waters teem with twenty-two different species of fish.

The Dead Sea is 47 miles long, 9½ miles at its greatest breadth and 1,300 feet at its greatest depth. It covers an area nearly 340 square miles. Since it lies nearly 1,300 feet below sea level, it has no outlet whatever. It is called "dead" because no organic life can exist in it due to the great amount of salt it contains.

Generally speaking, the climate of Palestine is that of all Mediterranean countries: hot, dry summers, wet but mild winters, though in the Jordan valley it is tropical. The heat is always bearable in the hill country. At sunset there is a considerable drop in temperature. Consequently, a cold night may succeed a day of torrid heat. Roughly speaking there are only two seasons, the hot and the cold, or the dry and the rainy season.

(Cf. Appendix I—*Plains, Seas, Mountains, and Rivers of the Holy Land*).

CHAPTER VI

SOME PARTICULAR CONSIDERATIONS OF THE OLD TESTAMENT

Old Testament Morality

THE following *objections* are made against the morality of the O. T.:

a) DECEPTION. Time and again lies and deception are recorded: Abraham deceived both Pharao and Abimelech asserting that he is traveling not with his wife, but with his sister (Gn 12:9-19; 20:1-8). Similar occurrences may be found in Gn 26:7-11; Gn 27:24; Jgs 4:11-22.

b) HUMAN SACRIFICE OCCURS. Jepthe immolates his daughter to God. (Jgs 11:29-40).

c) CRUELTY AND VIOLATION OF RIGHTS. The Jews showed cruelty and violation towards their enemies. (Cf. Dt 7:1-2; 20:10-18; Jos 9).

d) INDECENCY. The O. T. contains things which our minds abhor and consider indecent: v.g., Abraham's willingness to surrender his wife to Pharaoh and Abimelech (Gn 12:9f; 20:1f; 26:1f); Jacob's introduction of polygamy among the Hebrews and his novel

method of increasing his own flock (Gn 29:20; Cf.
also Gn 16:1f; 21:9ff; Gn 19:8; 19:30f; Gn 34:7f;
38:13f; Jgs 19; Ru 3; 1 Sm 18:27; 25:42-44; 2 Sm
3:2-5; 6:20-23; 5:13-16; 11:27; 3 Kgs. 1:3-4; 2 Sm
13:1f; Is 64:6; Ez 16:4; 16:15f; 23:2f; Gn 49:14;
Nu 23:22; Ps 77:65.

e) IMPRECATORY PSALMS. There are some psalms which
invoke the most drastic punishment on the enemies
of the Hebrews. (Cf. Ps 2:9).

REPLY: We must remember that mere mention of these
things by the O. T. writers does not mean that they approve
of them. A newspaper reporter or an historian does not
necessarily approve the crimes which he reports.

If God sometimes instructed the Jews to slay their
enemies, etc., He did so for a reason. Besides, God has full
dominion over life and death of all creatures. This does not
prove that God is cruel, but that He permits cruelty for a
time.

As to the other moral difficulties, we must bear in mind
that the Jews were often influenced by pagan environment
and pagan neighbors; they followed the trend of the times;
their knowledge of morality was not as refined and advanced
as is ours.

Longevity of the Patriarchs

The length of life attributed to the early men is indeed
surprising. "The shortest-lived in this list is Henoch whom
God took living from this world when he was 365 years old,
while of the remainder the average length of life was 900."[3]

"The great span of life attributed to the early representative of humanity presents a problem ... Some Catholic scholars have endeavored to solve the problem by reducing the numbers, or by asserting that year does not mean the period of twelve months. But these attempts are admittedly unsatisfactory ... It seems to be the conviction of the sacred author that the early patriarchs lived long. In Gn 47:9 Jacob replies to the question of the Pharaoh, 'The days of my pilgrimage are 130 years, few and evil, and they are not come up to the days of the pilgrimage of my father.' This is confirmed by the fact that the extra-biblical narratives also have indications of a longer duration of human life. There is nothing contradictory in this from the psysiological point of view; the body did not necessarily immediately lose all the energy that was conferred upon it by God, but only consequently upon the abuses of the 'Way of corruption' of the sons of Adam. An age much greater than that of the present could have been attained."[4] Recent opinions consider the figures as round or approximate or based on an artificial scheme. A more definitive answer to the problem cannot now be given.

Sacred Times and Festivals

Among the Jews a day was reckoned from sunset to sunset. The Jews' week of seven days was founded on the week of creation, the seventh day being a day of rest. Time was reckoned by moon and not by sun. The month corresponded to the period of the moon's circuit around the earth. A new month began with each new moon. The first of the month was a holy day in which special sacrifices were offered (Nu 28:11-15).

THE PASSOVER was the feast commemorating the liberation of the Jews from Egypt.

THE FEAST OF PENTECOST (from the Greek "pentecoste" meaning fiftieth day) was celebrated fifty days after the Passover. It was celebrated in thanksgiving for the corn and wheat harvest, and in commemoration of the giving of the Law on Mt. Sinai.

THE FEAST OF TABERNACLES was celebrated from the 15th to the 21st of the seventh month, Tishri. It commemorated the forty years of wandering in the desert and marked the end of the fruit, oil, and wine harvest.

THE DAY OF ATONEMENT was observed on the 10th of Tishri. It was a day of absolute fast, of repentance and sorrow for sin.

THE FEAST OF PURIM (lots) was celebrated on the 14th and 15th of the 12th month, Adar, to commemorate the salvation of the Jews by Esther when they were about to be destroyed through the plotting of Aman of the Persian Court. It got its name from the fact that Aman cast lots to determine the day on which to slay the Jews.

THE FEAST OF THE DEDICATION OF THE TEMPLE, celebrated on the 25th of Kisleu, commemorated the rededication of the temple after it had been desecrated by Antiochus of Syria.

Religious Sects and Groups

THE SCRIBES were the authorized interpreters and guardians of the Law who in a certain sense continued the work of the prophets.

THE PHARISEES were a sect of the Scribes. They were a class of men whose ambition was to keep themselves separate from the defiling contact of the Gentiles and from the ordinary multitude 'which knew not the law and was accursed' (Jn 7:49). They were the select groups, the "inner circle" within the holy people.

THE ZEALOTS were an offshoot of the Pharisees. They were a sort of extreme Jewish youth movement which carried nationalism to the verge of fanaticism.

THE PROSELYTES were converts from paganism to Judaism.

THE SADDUCEES were the Jewish aristocrats of the priestly caste. They were the freethinkers of Christ's time.

THE HERODIANS were the worldly and scheming admirers and followers of Herod who had more in common with the Sadducees than with the Pharisees.

THE SAMARITANS were a people of mixed origin, partly Jewish and partly Gentile. The Jews and the Samaritans were enemies.

THE NAZARITES were those who vowed to abstain from vinegar and liquors, to avoid touching or looking at dead bodies, even of relatives, and to let their hair and beard grow. They could take this vow for life or for a limited time, the minimum being thirty days.

THE PUBLICANS were men concerned with the public revenues. They were detested by the Jews because they endeavored to extort from the people not only the taxes but something over and above for themselves.

Chapter VII

THE HISTORICAL BOOKS OF THE OLD TESTAMENT

IN this chapter we will give a brief resume of each historical book of the O. T. mentioning, when possible, the author and date. Since this is only a brief aid to the Bible, we will consider only a few of the more important problems that might arise concerning certain passages. For a more detailed presentation books mentioned in the Bibliography might be consulted.

THE PENTATEUCH

The first five books of the O. T., the books of Moses, are called the "Pentateuch," a word which signifies a book composed of five rolls. The Pentateuch contains the religious history of the chosen people and of their ancestors from the creation of the first man to the death of Moses, and the laws, religious and social, of their theocratic system.

AUTHOR OF THE FIVE BOOKS. "It has long been recognized that the Pent. has not come down to us precisely as it left the hand of Moses and that apart from the errors of copyists it has received additions and modifications . . .So when the

Mosaic authorship is spoken of, it must be borne in mind that the authorship meant is that of the work as a whole with allowance for subsequent modifications."[5] Recent Catholic writers hold it is Mosaic in spirit and essence.

Biographical Note: Moses was born in Egypt, of the tribe of Levi, the third child of Amram and Jochabed.

At the time of his birth the decree was death for every newly born Hebrew male (Ex 1:16). His mother hid him among the bulrushes along the Nile where Pharao's daughter found and adopted him (Ex 2).

He was raised at the court of Pharao. When he was forty years old he slew an Egyptian in defense of a fellow Jew; as a result he had to flee. At Madian he married Sephore who bore him two sons, Gersam and Eliezer (Ex 2:11-22; Acts 7:25-29). After forty years of shepherding, God appeared to him in a burning bush, and ordered him to go to Pharao and demand the release of the Israelites. Moses took his brother Aaron as his spokesman. Pharao treated the Israelites more cruelly. By the power of God, Moses smote Egypt with ten plagues (Ex 7:12). Finally, Pharao permitted the Israelites to depart, but repenting his move, he pursued them. When Moses, with God's help, opened a passage in the Red Sea, the Israelites escaped, but the Egyptian pursuers were drowned when they tried to follow (Ex. 14).

For the next forty years, the Israelites wandered in search of the promised land. During this period Moses interceded for them many times, obtaining many miraculous benefits for them. During these wanderings, Moses received the Ten Commandments from God on Mt. Sinai (Ex 20). Because he doubted God's mercy towards the ever-rebellious Jews, Moses was not permitted to enter the Promised Land (Nu 20: 7-13). He died at the age of one hundred and twenty after having seen the Promised Land from Mount Nebo (Dt 34).

Genesis

The first Mosaic book, Genesis, receives its name from the Greek word which means "becoming, beginning, coming into being," i.e., the book tells of the origin of the world and of Israel.

Contents: This book contains the creation of the world and of our first parents, Adam and Eve; the origin of sin in the fall of our first parents; the deluge—Noe and his family being saved in the ark; the Tower of Babel and the dispersion of the human race (Chapters 1-11); the call of Abraham, the Father of the Chosen People (12-25:18); the birth and marriage of Abraham's son, Isaac, (25:19-26); the birth of Isaac's sons, Esau and Jacob, and the disagreement between them (25-28); the account of Jacob and his twelve sons (28-36); the story of Joseph and his brothers; the descent of Jacob (also called "Israel") and his brethren into Egypt, which begins the sojourn of the Jews in Egypt (37-50).

SOME PARTICULAR CONSIDERATIONS: (1:1-25) *Creation of the World:* Here we have a popular account of the world as conceived by the ancient Hebrews in accordance with appearances. "The purpose of the sacred writer was to give his contemporaries a clear knowledge of the fact of the creation of all things by the One True God, and to convey this knowledge in the language of his time and in a manner accommodated to the then popular ideas of the structure of the universe. The statement of the creation, then, is strictly historical. The language is popular, not scientific. The division into day (in the Hexaemeron) and the succession of the several acts of creation are a literary device employed by the sacred author to make his account intelligible to his first readers, or at least to bring it home to their minds in a striking and vivid manner."[6]

Anthropomorphism (1:26) is the attributing to God the forms, organs, operations, and general characteristics of human nature. Here God is envisioned as consulting with Himself.

Day of Rest (2:3): Moses employed a period of a week for the creation to impress upon the Jews the fact that the seventh day of the week was holy and a day of rest. Catholic exegetes are unanimous in rejecting the old theory that God accomplished everything in the space of six twenty-four hour periods.

Creation of Man (2:4f): "The Biblical description of how God made the first man is highly anthropomorphic. Yahweh (God) fashions a body from the earth and breathes into its nose life-giving breath. Because he was made from the earth, 'adamah', and returns again to earth, the first man was named Adam. The life-giving breath of animals also proceeds from God. But there exists a fundamental difference between man and animal; endowed with intelligence, man is immeasurably superior to animals; he shows this by imposing names upon them... In all essential points the Genesis account is historical. But a distinction must be made between religious doctrine and the dress in which it is presented. Doubtlessly the sacred author wished to teach that man's body takes its origin from the earth and therefore is mortal, while the soul is essentially different from the body. The human soul, being endowed with reason, can be brought into existence only through a special, divine creative act; it could not have evolved by a purely natural process from an animal soul."[7]

Garden of Eden (2:8f): "Eden may be Bit-Adini on the middle Euphrates, or, perhaps more probably, may represent the Assyrian word *edinu,* meaning an open plain or desert, as that is what the territory was in which the garden was situated."[8]

"The Tree of Life (2:9): is probably to be conceived as having fruit of preternatural power capable of entirely restoring human energy and vitality and so of preserving the strength of youth. By its means Adam and Eve, though mortal by nature, would have enjoyed the gift of immortality."[9]

"The Tree of Knowledge of Good and Evil (2:17): is so called because through it Adam gained experimental knowledge of good and evil; after eating the fruit of it, he learned how good it was to obey God, and how evil to disobey him."[10] Some Catholic scholars consider the Trees as metaphors for ideas.

Formation of Eve (2:21f): "According to a decree of the Biblical Commission, the doctrine of the 'formation of the first woman from man' must be maintained. But the exact way in which it took place remains a mystery 'about which you are able to say nothing; for only that One knows who was responsible for creation.' "11

Temptation and Fall (3:1-24); *Serpent* (3:1): Either Satan entered into a serpent or he assumed the external appearance of a snake, or the snake is the symbol of Satan. *Fruit* (3:6): Scripture makes no mention of an apple. In fact, no particular fruit is mentioned. *Nature of the Sin:* The sin was not against sex. It was an act of disobedience proceeding from pride, for Adam and Eve sought to be like God.

The Protoevangel (3:15): This passage is so called, i.e., First Gospel, because here allusion is first made in the Bible of the Redeemer, Jesus Christ. In the Douay-Rheims version, the second part of this verse reads: "she shall crush thy head, and thou shalt lie in wait for her heel." The latest Catholic versions have: "He shall crush. . ., and you shall. . . for his heel." The "He" refers to Christ, the seed of the woman.

The Ark (6:14): The ark was not a maneuverable ship but rather a huge box. It satisfied requirements if it could float and if it had considerable storage room. If we assume that the Babylonian cubit was roughly 21 inches, then we could conclude that the ark was 525 feet long, 87½ feet broad, and 52½ feet high. It consisted of three decks and received light and air from a sort of casement of one cubit (i.e., 1 and ¾ feet) in height which ran around the sides of the ship a little below the roof. In 1609 Peter Jansen of Horn, Holland, building a vessel of the same proportions, found that it would stow one third more cargo than other ships of ordinary structure.

Extent of the Flood (7:20f): What was the extent of

the flood? "To this question three answers have been suggested: 1) the flood was geographically universal, i.e., it covered the surface of the entire earth, and destroyed all living things except those in the ark; 2) it was not geographically universal but anthropologically universal, i.e., only that part of the earth that was inhabited by man was inundated, so that the entire human race outside the ark perished; (not all the animals, however, since it was geographically limited); 3) it was neither geographically nor anthropologically universal, but was limited to a certain region, and all men inhabiting that region perished."[12] Of these the second and the third opinions are probable.

Tower of Babel (11:1f): It is certain that all living men were not at the Tower of Babel. Nor can this account mean that this was the only cause of the diversity of languages. We must remember that the different groups among the Japhethites and Chamites (Gn 10:5, 20) and among the Semites (Gn 10:31) are already said to have their own various languages. What the sacred author means is that the people who were in complete harmony at first, argued among themselves and could not agree upon a common policy. As a result of this discord, there was migration. The moral lesson of the story is the downfall of man's pride.

Destruction of Sodom and Gomorra (19:23f): God often makes use of natural means to carry out His purposes. "The cause of the disaster was probably the escape through earthquake action of compressed gases and petroleum from the subterranean deposits in the neighborhood of the doomed cities. Spontaneous combustion is apt to occur in such circumstances, and domestic fires would quickly ignite the escaping gases and oil. Such a fire would cause immense clouds of smoke (vs. 28)."[13] God thus used natural means to carry out the much deserved punishment.

Punishment of Lot's Wife (19:26): Lot's wife was probably overwhelmed by the fumes, and later her body became incrusted with salt, thus making her look like a "pillar of salt." "The casts of human bodies preserved in the museum of Pompei suggests what happened to Lot's wife. These casts preserve the exact form of the victims who were overwhelmed by the eruption and became encased in the falling ashes."[14]

Exodus

The second book of the Pentateuch is called Exodus from the Greek word for "departure" because the main event narrated in it is the departure of the Israelites from Egypt.

Contents: Exodus contains the account of the oppression of the Jews; the birth, adoption, call, and mission of Moses (1-7:13); the ten plagues which God sent upon the Egyptians to bring about the release of the Jews (7:14 12:36); the departure of the Jews from Egypt (12:37; 14: 22); the destruction of the pursuing Egyptians by drowning (14:23f); the experiences and miraculous occurrences during the journey (15-19); the giving of the ten Commandments and other laws (20-24); the setting up and furnishing of God's house, the tabernacle (25-31); the adoration of the golden calf by the Jews, the breaking of the tablets containing the Commandments, and the atonement of the people (32); more religious laws and regulations concerning the house of God (34-40).

SOME PARTICULAR CONSIDERATIONS: *The First Nine Plagues* (7:14-10): "The first nine plagues, viz., the Nile water changing into blood, frogs, mosquitoes, gnats, cattle murrain, boils, locusts, darkness, have parallels in natural phenomena proper to Egypt and occurring occasionally in the delta. Nevertheless, the Biblical plagues do not represent a case of mere natural phenomena because: a) they were predicted by Moses, b) they began at his word and ceased as he foretold, c) there exists no record of similar phenomena of like intensity."[15]

The Tenth Plague: The Death of the First-born (11-12): "The Lord slew every first-born of Pharao on the throne to the first-born of the prisoner in the dungeon, as well as all the first-born of the animals." (12:29). The Israelites were spared after each family killed a lamb, smeared the lintels and door-posts with its blood, and ate the flesh as a sacrificial meal in obedience to God's command. This was the first feast of the Passover. The practice of dedicating the first-born to God was inaugurated at this time.

Crossing of the Red Sea (14:10f): "We are told that a steady and strong east wind caused the waters to be separated toward the north and south, and dried the stretch of land between. The fact the bed dried so quickly, and that women and children and caravans could cross indicates that the gulf was shallow in this section. The rocky formation of the bed enabled it to dry quickly with the aid of the warm wind. The Egyptians undoubtedly being familiar with the region presumed that the same conditions would remain unchanged until they also crossed. They could estimate the climate, but they could not estimate the Divine Will. With the subsiding of the wind, the waters began to return to their natural place, first beneath the sands, causing a quick-sand in which the chariots sank, and then as the space was again occupied by the waters, the army would be submerged. The miracle consisted in God's disposal of natural causes to a determined end. The primary cause was God, the secondary physical forces."[16] Father Bandas writes that "at Suez, the tide together with a strong wind has been seen to drive back the Sea for a considerable distance. A strong wind has been known to make the waters of Lake Menzaleh (at the Mediterranean entrance to the Suez Canal) recede for a distance of seven miles. Something similar was observed in Crimea in 1738."[17] "The crossing was not miraculous in itself since the natural force of the wind divided the waters of the ford... But it was miraculous in the intensity and con-tinuity of the wind, in the circumstances of time and place and in the pillars of cloud and fire by which the Israelites were accompanied."[18]

The Quail and Manna (16:4f): In the springtime, *quails* from the interior of Africa fly over the Sinaitic peninsula in large numbers. That they came later in May and even in June and were so numerous on the second occasion as to provide a month's food for all the people is indicative of divine intervention.

"The *manna* differed from the quails in being supplied constantly during the whole period of the wandering in the desert. This continuous and miraculous provision of food was a signal prodigy worked by Yahweh on behalf of His people. The bread from heaven was thus a most fitting type of the true bread from heaven, the sacrament of the Eucha-rist, our spiritual food during our journey to the Promised Land. The manna however was not entirely preternatural.

A substance found beneath the tamarisk trees in Sinai in late May, June, and July is called manna by the natives. In an expedition to Sinai in 1927, two professors of the Hebrew University of Jerusalem discovered that it was produced not by the tamarisk tree itself but by two species of cochineal which feed on its leaves. The viscous substance falls to the ground during the night and appears in the morning in the form of little balls never bigger than a hazel-nut and usually of yellow brown color and transparent. It must be collected early since ants appear after 8:30 A.M., and devour or carry away what they find. Once hardened it neither melts under the heat of the sun nor becomes in any way corrupt. As its contents is mainly sugar it is very nourishing. The present annual output in Sinai is about 6 cwt., (hundredweight is a unit of weight equal to 100 pounds in the U.S.), but the ancient yield was greater since there were more tamarisks. The biblical narrative here and Nu 11:7-9 agrees with this description. The manna is food from heaven (4) as coming from above and also miraculously multiplied since the natural supply was altogether insufficient... The *corruption* of the manna (20) was a miracle by which the people were warned to obey God and trust in Him. Its *melting* when the sun grew hot cannot be explained by the ravages of the ants, since "melt" and "disappear" are not equivalent, but the drops which fell from the trees during the day time would melt in the sun before they solidified (21). The manna was either eaten raw or cooked. A miracle is necessary to explain the extraordinary large amount provided and also the double supply on the eve of the Sabbath."[19]

The Ten Commandments (20:1f): The first three commandments prescribe man's duty to God, the remaining seven his duty to his neighbor.

The Golden Calf (32:1f): After the ratification of the covenant Moses reascended the mountain and remained there forty days and forty nights (24:18). After a time the people imagined he would not return and they wanted an image of Yahweh, their God and Leader. At their petition, Aaron made a golden bull which throughout the Orient was an accepted symbol of divinity. It is thought by some that the golden calf was intended as an image of the Lord Himself, not of a false god. The strength of a young bull signified God's strength. The Israelites, however, had been forbidden to represent the Lord under any visible form.

Leviticus

The name of this book comes from its ancient translators who gave it such a name because a considerable part of it is concerned with the religious duties of the priests of the tribe of Levi.

Contents: The main divisions of this book are concerned with: 1) laws of sacrifice (1-7); 2) the ceremony of ordination of Aaron and his sons (8-10); the laws of purification (legal purity) (11-15); the Day of Atonement (16); the laws of legal holiness, which gave many regulations concerning the daily life of the Israelites, feasts, etc. (17-26); regulations concerning vows and tithes (27).

Numbers

This book takes its name from the fact that it contains accounts of the taking of two censuses of the Hebrew people (i.e., the "numbers" of them), one at the beginning and one at the end of their forty years of wandering in the desert.

Contents: This book opens with a description of the census of the Israelites, the arrangement of the tribes in their camps, and the duties of the Levites, who are to take the place of the first born of the children of Israel in the divine services in the temple (1-4); more laws and regulations are then enumerated (5-8); the second Passover is recalled (9); the many years of wandering from Mt. Sinai to the plain of Moab are related, together with the murmurings and revolts against God, and the punishment imposed upon and the mercy of God shown to the Israelites (10-22); the sojourn in the plains of Moab, the appointment of Josue as Moses' successor, the plans of the Israelites to enter into Canaan, the promised land, and to divide it among the tribes and Levites are described in the remaining chapters (22-36).

Deuteronomy

Deuteronomy means "Second Law." This title is due to a mistranslation of 17:18. Actually, it does not contain a second law, but rather an elucidation of the former laws. This is the last of the five books of Moses.

Contents: This book contains the great discourses of Moses to the Israelites. The two introductory discourses of Moses comprise chapters 1-11; the principal laws of the Israelites are next reviewed and the people encouraged to obey them under threat of dire punishment for transgressions (12-26); the final words of Moses are then recorded (27-30); the final chapters (31-34) are concerned with instructions to Josue, Moses' successor; the beautiful canticle of Moses; the blessing of the tribes; and the death and burial of Moses.

Chapter VIII

THE HISTORICAL BOOKS OF THE OLD TESTAMENT
(Continued)

Josue

THIS book derives its name from Moses' successor, Josue, about whom it is principally concerned.

"The actual author of the book in its present form remains unknown. Many indications point to a date of composition prior to King David's reign; and some of the detailed description, which seems to have been composed by an eyewitness, may even be the work of Josue himself."[20]

The Contents: The following main events are contained in this book: the miraculous crossing of the Jordan; the fall of Jericho, the conquest of Canaan, the promised land (1-12); the division of the land among the twelve tribes of Israel (13-22); the final admonitions and instructions of Josue, and his death (23-24).

SOME PARTICULAR CONSIDERATIONS. *Crossing of the Jordan* (3:14f): "Though the sudden damming of the river may have been caused directly by a land-slide, as has happened on other occasions, yet the miraculous character of the present event is not thereby removed. God, who foretold the event (3:13), could cause it to take place at precisely the right moment (3:15). Nevertheless, the account seems to favor an immediate intervention of God."[21]

Capture of Jericho (6:1f): "The wall collapsed by the miraculous intervention of God, who may have used an earthquake for this purpose. The blowing of the horns and the shouting of the people, which obviously of themselves could not have produced this effect, were intended by God as a test of the people's obedience and of their faith in His promise; cf. Heb 11:30."

"Garstang's excavations have illustrated and confirmed many details of the biblical narrative. The city captured by Josue was about five acres in extent and had a double wall of brick about 650 yards in circumference so that seven rounds of the walls could be made in a few hours. Many houses were observed built up against the city wall like Rahab's. This wall, 12 feet thick, collapsed outwardly into the space between the two walls. The outer wall, 6 feet thick, fell down the slope of the hill. The uncovering of the stone foundations showed that neither wall had been undermined. The walls wherever disclosed 'are found to be deeply fissured and as it were dislocated. The indications point to earthquake' (Garstang). If God used this natural means, the providential determination of time and place would still be miraculous. The ruins show traces of deliberate incendiarism. Garstang dates the catastrophe 1400-1388, Vincent 1250-1200 B.C."[23] Excavations have been resumed recently, and the whole question of Jericho is again an open one.

"Great stones from the sky" (10:11): These were hailstones.

"The sun halted in the middle of the sky" (10:13): By a miracle unique in history the day was prolonged to twice its ordinary length. In calling upon the sun "to stand still," Josue spoke in popular language since we know that scientifically speaking the earth moves and not the sun.

Judges

The Book of Judges receives its title from the twelve heroes of Israel whose deeds it records. These military leaders (not magistrates) were sent by God to aid and to relieve His people in time of external danger. Because six of them—Othoniel, Aod, Barar, Gedeon, Jepthe, and Samson are treated in some detail they have been styled the MAJOR JUDGES. The other six (Samgar, Thola, Ahialon, Jair, Abesan, and Abdon), about whom only a summary record is given, are called the MINOR JUDGES. There are two other judges, whose judgeships are described in 1 Samuel—Heli and Samuel, who seemed to have ruled the entire nation of Israel just before the institution of the monarchy. The twelve judges of the present book, however, probably exercised their authority, sometimes simultaneously, over one or another tribe of Israel, but never over the entire nation.

Contents: This book covers the history of the Jews from Josue to Samuel, the last of the Judges. Chapters 1 & 2 give a description of the infidelity and idolatry of the Israelites after the death of Josue; chapters 3 to 16 contain biographical sketches of the Judges who ruled Israel; chapters 17 to

21 are concerned with the tribes of Dan and Benjamin in the days of the Judges.

SOME PARTICULAR CONSIDERATIONS: *Jephte's Vow* (11: 30): The text clearly shows that Jephte vowed a human sacrifice, according to the custom of his pagan neighbors. His vow was objectively immoral, and in carrying it out, as the account would lead us to believe, Jephte was objectively sinning. However, because of his ignorance, he was probably free from any subjective guilt. The inspired author merely records the fact of Jephte's vow; he does not approve the action.

"Mourn my virginity" (11:37): To bear children was a woman's greatest pride, and to be childless was regarded as a great misfortune. Here Jephte's daughter asks for two months to mourn the fact that she will be put to death before she can bear children.

"Water issued from it" (15:19): Water came from the mortar, which was a circular depression in the rock; it did not come from the jawbone.

"If I am shaved, my strength will leave me" (16:17): "The strength of Samson was not in his hair. The long uncut lock was a sign of his consecration to God according to the rite of the Nazarite (cf. Ch. VI, Sec. IV). His strength came from God in virtue of his consecration to Him. When his lust drew him away from God, Samson lost the sign of his consecration and the consecration with its accompanying strength."[24]

"He pushed hard, etc." (16:30): By displacing the wooden pillars at the entrance of the temple, he caused the building to collapse.

Ruth

This book takes its name from Ruth, the Moabite woman, about whom it is mostly concerned.

There is no certainty about the author of this book which was written long after the events had occurred (4:7). The events took place "in the time of the Judges" (1:1).

Contents: The four chapters of this book tell how Ruth, a Moabite woman, after the death of her Jewish husband, returned with her mother-in-law, Noemi, to the latter's former home in Judea. Here Ruth married Booz of the tribe of Benjamin. Ruth gave birth to Obed, the grandfather of David. This made her an ancestress of David and of Christ.

1 & 2 Samuel (1 & 2 Kings)

These books are named after Samuel because they contain the history of Samuel and the two kings, Saul and David, whom he anointed kings of Israel.

A single author, using older materials, composed these two books together with the following two books (3 & 4 Kings) shortly after the deportation of 586. The writer is not Jeremias, but someone who came under his influence.

Contents: 1 SAMUEL. This book gives us the history of Samuel, the last of the judges, and the account of Heli and his two sons. It tells of the battles with the Philistines, the wanderings of the ark of the covenant, and how Samuel meets Saul while the latter is looking for his father's animals. It describes how Samuel anoints Saul first king of the Israelites and explains the sign which God used to show His chosen people His displeasure at their requesting a king (1-12). Chapters 13-18 narrate the establishment of the Jewish kingdom with Saul as king; Saul's disobedience to God's command for which he was cast off by the Lord; the anointing of David by Samuel; the slaying of the giant Goliath by David; the envy of Saul and his designs upon David's life. Chapters 19-31 tell of the many attempts of Saul and his men on David's life; recount the Philistine war against the Israelites; mention other experiences of David; describe the defeat of the Israelites by the Philistines, and the slaying of Saul and his sons.

2 SAMUEL. In Chapters 1-7: David mourns Saul's death; he is anointed king of Juda and later king of all Israel; he defeats the Philistines; David brings the ark from Cariathiarim to his house, and plans to build a temple. In Chapters 8-18: David's victories are mentioned; David commits adultery with Bethsabee, and not finding any means to conceal it, causes her husband to be slain; David confesses his sins, and is forgiven, but must endure punishment; family problems and the treachery of Absalom are told; David is forced to flee; the death of Absalom is recounted. Other acts of David as king are narrated in the remaining chapters (18-24).

3 & 4 Kings

These two books are called 3 & 4 Kings by Catholics, but the Hebrews call them 1 & 2 Kings. They contain the history of the Kingdoms of Israel and Juda from the reign of Solomon to the captivity.

Contents: 3 KINGS. This book tells of the death of David and the succession of his son, Solomon, to the throne. It describes the wisdom and riches of Solomon; tells of the building and the dedication of the temple in Jerusalem; recounts Solomon's sin of idolatry and his death (1-11). It narrates the split of the Jewish kingdom into the Northern and Southern kingdoms—the latter comprising the tribes of Benjamin and Juda (the Kingdom of Juda), and the former consisting of the other ten tribes (the Kingdom of Israel). The parallel histories of both kingdoms are related, concluding with the remarkable deeds of the prophet Elias (12-22).

4 KINGS. The twenty-five chapters of this book describe the accomplishments of the prophet, Eliseus; continue the parallel histories of the Northern and Southern kingdoms; record the fall of the Northern Kingdom of Israel in 722 B.C., when the ten tribes were taken into captivity by the Assyrians, and the end of the Southern Kingdom of Juda in 586 B.C., when the Babylonians carried the tribes of Benjamin and Juda into captivity.

1 & 2 *Paralipomenon*

The word "paralipomenon" comes from the Greek meaning "things left over." The Septuagint and the Vulgate employ this title, "a circumstance which would seem to present them (1 & 2 Par) merely as a supplement to the historical

books which preceded them." The Hebrews called them
"Chronicles."

The interest manifest in the Levites, including the
singers and doorkeepers suggests that the author was a
Levite. The composition of these books must be dated after
the conquest of Palestine by Alexander the Great in 331.

Contents: 1 PARALIPOMENON stresses ancient genealogies
(1-9) and concentrates on the history of Saul (10) and
David (11-29).

2 PARALIPOMENON is concerned with the history of
Solomon (1-9) and the kings of the Southern Kingdoms
(10-36). In chapter 36:23 mention is made of the release
of the Jews from Babylonian captivity by Cyrus.

Esdras and Nehemias (2 Esdras)

In the early Hebrew Bible, Esdras and Nehemias form
one book entitled "The Book of Esdras." In the Vulgate
they are known as "1 & 2 Esdras." We will accept the Confraternity designation and call the first book "Esdras" and
the second "Nehemias."

Esdras gets its name from the holy Doctor of the Law,
Esdras, who led a group of Exiles back to Jerusalem (7-10).
Nehemias takes its name from the former servant of the
Persian king, who became a worthy governor of Juda after
the exile.

Contents: ESDRAS. Chapters 1 to 6 tell of the home-
coming of the Jews under Zorobabel and Josue after Cyrus

released them from Babylon. They tell how Cyrus restored the sacred vessels which Nabuchodonosor had stolen, and how Cyrus gave permission for the rebuilding of the temple. The number of Jews who returned is mentioned. In chapters 7 to 10 the second home-coming of the exiles under Esdras is recounted and the works of Esdras in Jerusalem are recorded.

NEHEMIAS. This book contains the history of the Jews after the return from captivity. It tells of the arrival of Nehemias, former servant of the King of Persia, who urges the rebuilding of Jerusalem's walls, and recounts the completion of the walls (1-7). The remaining chapters (8-13) explain the religious reforms inaugurated by Esdras and Nehemias.

Tobias

It cannot be determined whether the author was a native of Palestine or a Jew of the Diaspora (dispersion). This book was probably written about the year 200 B.C.

Contents: The fourteen chapters of this book are concerned with a certain Tobias, of the tribe of Nephtali, who is carried off with his wife and son (also called "Tobias") to Ninive during the Assyrian invasion of Palestine. He is noted for his fidelity to the Law and for his works of mercy. Although tried by tribulations, loss of fortune and blindness, he continues to trust in God for which he was later rewarded. Tobias sends his son to Rages in Media to collect a large sum of money which he has lent to a certain Gabelus.

The Archangel Gabriel, sent by God to accompany the young Tobias, helps him to find a wife, Sara, and to obtain the money from Gabelus.

Judith

This book received the name from its heroine.

"The intimate knowledge of the topography of Canaan and the fact that the book was probably written in Hebrew point to a Palestinian Jew as the author. As regards the date of writing it was certainly much later than the dates of the events recorded because there is mention of the death of Judith and the descendants of Achior (14:6; 16:30). Nothing further can be deduced with certainty."[25]

Contents: The sixteen chapters of this book tell how Judith, a rich and beautiful widow, on hearing that the citizens of Bethulia are considering surrender to Holofernes, who is besieging their city, enters Holofernes' camp, and when he becomes drunk cuts off his head, and thus saves her people from destruction.

Esther

This book receives its name from the woman who saved her countrymen from the death planned for them by Aman, the prime minister of King Assuerus.

Early commentators ascribed the book to Mardochai. Many modern Catholic scholars attribute it to a Jew living in

Persia, who made use of Mardochai's memoirs. Some Catholic scholars attribute a greater part of the book to Mardochai. For all practical purposes, the author is unknown. The book was probably written in Persia at the end of the fifth century B. C.

Contents: The sixteen chapters of this book tell how the Jewess, Esther, living in Babylonian exile with her uncle, Mardochai, was chosen by Assuerus to replace queen Vashti, who was deposed for disobedience. When Aman, the first minister of the king, to satisfy his resentment against Mardochai, petitions the king successfully to have all the Jews in the Empire put to death in a single day, Esther, at her uncle's instigation, denounces Aman's evil intentions to the king. Aman is put to death; Mardochai inherits his office; and the Jews obtain permission to slay their enemies. This is the origin of the feast of Purim (i. e. feast of Lots.)

1 *Machabees*

This and the following book (2 Machabees) are so called because they continue the history of the Jewish people under Judas Machabeus and his brothers. These are the last two books of the O. T.

The author, clearly a devout and believing Jew, with a first-hand knowledge of Palestine, probably wrote this book much later than the reign of John Hyrcanus, who died in 103 B. C.

Contents: Introductory chapters 1 and 2 deal with the death of Alexander the Great and the division of his empire, the persecution of Antiochus Epiphanes, and the revolt of the Machabees. Chapters 3 to 9:22 narrate the struggles of Judas against the Syrian generals, Appolonius, Seron, Gorgias, Lysias and Nicanor, all of whom he defeated. Next are related the purifying of the temple, Judas' treaty with the Romans, and his death on the battlefield of Elasa. In 9:23-12:54 are recounted the deeds and death of Jonathan. From chapters 12 to 16, the author recounts the deeds of Simon, who brings about the independence of Juda and who is proclaimed high priest, general, and ethnarch. The book concludes with an account of Simon's assassination and the succession of his son, John Hyrcanus.

2   M a c h a b e e s

The author of this book states that he is summarizing the five books of Jason of Cyrene (2:24). This book was probably written around 100 B. C.

Contents: The book narrates and supplements many of the facts mentioned in 1 Mc. In 1-2:19 are contained two letters sent from Jerusalem to the Jews of Egypt, urging them to celebrate the Feast of the Dedication. In chapters 3 to 7 are described the beginning of the persecutions, the profanation of the temple, the martyrdom of Eleazer and the seven sons and their mother. In chapters 8 to 15 are described the wars and victories of Judas Machabeus.

Chapter IX

DIDACTIC BOOKS OF THE OLD TESTAMENT

THE didactic books of the O. T. are those that are concerned with doctrinal truths, principles of morality, and the inculcation of a way of life. These might be expressed in poetical form, e.g., the Psalms, or in prose, e.g., Proverbs. The didactic books of the O. T. are: Job, Psalms, Proverbs, Ecclesiastes, Canticle of Canticles, Wisdom and Sirach (Ecclesiasticus).

Job

This book takes its name from its chief character. The author, who was a well-educated and well-traveled Palestinian Jew, is unknown. The work may have appeared about 450 or 500 B. C., and the discourses of Elihu (32-37) were added some time later.

Contents: The forty-two chapters of this book tell of Job, who lived in the land of Hus, in the northern part of Palestine. He was the wealthy head of a large clan, possessing lands and cattle in abundance. In rapid succession he lost everything, and was afflicted with a loathsome disease, so that he became an outcast from his own people. His friends tell him that his suffering is sent by God because of his sins and that he must repent. Job agrees that afflictions come from God, and that God afflicts those who are guilty of sin, but at the same time, Job is not conscious of sin. Elihu, the Buzite, offers a new solution to the problem of evil. He says that sin is not the only cause of suffering. Suffering may be sent by God as a means of probation and purification for higher glory.

God finally intervenes, showing Job that it is folly to question divine providence, but at the same time commending Job for not accepting the false solutions of his friends.

The Psalms

The Psalter, i.e., the book of Psalms, is the inspired hymnal of the O. T. Christ used the psalms in prayer and His Church has followed His example.

The word "psalm" comes from the Greek "psalmos" or "psallein" which denotes a sacred song to be sung to the accompaniment of a stringed instrument.

There are 150 psalms in the Psalter. However, the numbering of the psalms differ in the Catholic and Protestant versions. This is due to the way the psalms have been divided.

In the Apostolic Letter, "In Cotidianis Precibus" of March 24, 1945, Pope Pius XII permitted the use of the Psalter translated from the Hebrew by the Pontifical Biblical Institute in the recitation of the Breviary.

The Psalter is divided into five books which are separated one from the other by a doxology:

1—Pss.	1- 40	4—Pss.	89-105
2—Pss.	41- 71	5—Pss.	106-150
3—Pss.	72- 88		

Many of the psalms begin with a title, e.g., A Psalm of David.

"Bearing in mind that the titles represent a very ancient tradition, it would be rash to disregard their evidence when they give the composers of the hymns. Psalms are attributed to Moses (89), Solomon (71, 126), the sons of Core (41-48,-83, 84, 86), Eman (87), Ethan (88), Asaph, (49, 72-82), and probably Idithun (38, 61-76); but by far the largest attribution is to David (73 in the Hebrew text; 84 psalms in the Septuagint) . . . David, therefore, was Israel's best known hymn writer. It is not improbable that besides composing psalms he also re-edited ancient liturgical hymns; a clear example of editing is 67, where we have a combination of at least 3 sacred songs.

"And it is not too much to expect that eventually the psalms may be shown to be a magnificent collection of poems reaching from the time of the Exodus right up to the Maccabean period."[26]

Contents: The psalms may be divided into the following categories:

DIDACTIC—which treat of God's attributes and His relation to man (1, 36, 48, 72);

HISTORICAL—which concern some historical incident (3, 17, 26);

NATIONAL—which treat of the history of the chosen people (77, 78, 104, 105);

FESTAL—sung at the religious feasts and services (14, 23, 112, 117);

GRADUAL—sung by the pilgrims on their way to Jerusalem and by the singers on the steps of the temple (119-133);

MESSIANIC—pertaining to the future Messias (2, 21, 68, 109);

PENITENTIAL—containing thoughts of contrition for sin (6, 31, 37, 50, 51, 129, 142).

VINDICTIVE—imploring punishment upon the enemies of God's chosen people (108);

LITURGICAL—containing words of the Jewish liturgy (66, 104, 133, 135, 148-150);

ALPHABETICAL OR ACROSTIC—because in the original each half verse, or verse, or every two verses, etc., began with a consecutive letter of the alphabet, perhaps as an aid to memory (9, 24, 33, 110, 111).

Proverbs

The word "proverbs" has a very wide meaning in Scripture—signifying moral saying, maxim, exhortation, parable, riddle or by-word. Often it refers to maxims expressed in poetic rhythm and concerned with moral instructions.

Proverbs contains the teachings of several wise men who lived in various periods. Included among these men and mentioned in the text itself are Solomon, Agur, and King Lamuel; nothing is known about the latter two. This book probably had its beginning in 800 B. C. and reached its completion in the fourth century B.C.

Contents: This book consists of an invitation to acquire wisdom (1: 8-9: 18); a collection of Solomon's proverbs (10: 1-22:16); a collection of sayings of the wise men (22:17-24: 34); another collection of the proverbs of Solomon (25:1-29:27); the sayings of Agur (30:1-14); the numerical sayings (30:15-33); the sayings of King Lamuel (31:1-9); a portrait of a virtuous wife (31:10-31).

E c c l e s i a s t e s

Ecclesiastes means "the preacher." This book has been considered a difficult book.

No longer do Catholic exegetes attribute this book to Solomon. "It seems then that the writer, part of whose purpose was to point out that earthly goods are unsatisfying, chose to impersonate Solomon, since he above all others was noted for all those possessions which seem to make for happiness. The words of such a one as Solomon would enforce most effectively the teaching that material prosperity is unsatisfactory."[27] The date for this book may be fixed somewhere towards the close of the third century B.C.

Contents: This book may be said to present two main thoughts: What is able to bring a permanent happiness in this world? Because man is short-lived and mortal, permanent and unchangeable, happiness cannot be obtained in this world (1-4:16). In chapters 4:17 to 12:14 the author points out what man must do to obtain happiness.

Canticle of Canticles

This book, whose full Hebrew title is "The Song of Songs, which is Solomon's," is called "Canticle of Canticles" because it is "the most excellent of all canticles." "It is indeed a most beautiful poem both for its lyrical inspiration and rich imagery as well as for the loftiness of its meaning."[28]

Although the Canticle of Canticles is attributed to Solomon in the same manner as the book of Ecclesiastes is attributed to him (cf. above), actually the author is unknown. The date of composition may be placed in the third or fourth century B. C.

Contents: This canticle of eight chapters is a love song in which two young shepherds praise each other's beauty and express their mutual love and desire for an indissoluble union.

Wisdom

In the Greek and Syriac Bibles this book is entitled: "The Wisdom of Solomon."

The author of this book was a Hellenistic Jew of the Diaspora (Dispersion) who wrote it in Greek probably between 150 and 50 B. C.

Contents: This book may be divided into two sections: didactic and historical. The didactic part (1-9) tells of the error and punishment of the sinner; the hope and rewards of the good and the confusion and punishment of the sinner; the obtaining of wisdom by prayer, and the properties and fruits of wisdom. The historical part (6-19) demonstrates from sacred history the consequences of wisdom, and how, because of it, God rewards the good and punishes the wicked —dealing specifically with idolatry and the deliverance of Israel.

Ecclesiasticus (Sirach)

In Hebrew this book is called "Ben Sira" (son of Sira) from the name of its author. The Greek version calls it "The Wisdom of Jesus, son of Sirach." Among the early Christians the title commonly used was "Ecclesiasticus Liber" (church book). The Church used this book frequently in her public readings and in her instructions to prospective converts.

The author, Jesus, son of Sirach, was from Jerusalem. The book was written 190-180 B. C.

Contents: This book aims to point out a way of life for those who seek wisdom and strive to live according to the Divine Law. In its moral section (1-43) the rules for the practice of virtue are laid down. In its historical part (44-50) the wisdom of the great men of the O. T., is illustrated. Chapter 51 concludes the book with a prayer of praise and thanksgiving.

CHAPTER *X*

PROPHETICAL BOOKS OF THE OLD TESTAMENT

Notion of Prophet

A prophet is a person who speaks in the name of God, or who acts as His interpreter. The prophets were the spokesmen of God and communicated God's messages—past, present, and future—to men. Besides predicting the future, the prophets of Israel also served as the religious leaders and teachers of the Jews. Some of the prophets also played an important part in the political and public life of their nation, a fact that is quite understandable when we realize that in Israel politics and religion were intimately interwoven.

The Channels of Prophecy

"Revelation came to the prophets in three ways: a) by an *external image* perceived by the senses of the prophet; for example, the burning bush of Moses or the handwriting on the wall of Balthasar's banquet hall; b) by an *internal image* perceived by the prophet in a vision, dream or ecstasy; c) by *words* spoken directly to the prophet. The prophets frequently explained the message to the people or acted it out for them. The gift of prophecy was not habitual to them. They were not in constant communication with God. They distinguished their own concepts from the contents of the divine message, and when they had no illumination from God they were fully aware of the fact."[29]

Authority of the Prophets

The *true prophets* were known by their irreproachable characters and conduct; by the miracles they performed in the confirmation of their teaching; by the fact that their predictions came true, etc.

"The *false prophets,* on the other hand, were actuated by base motives, corrupted by pride, made fantastic predictions, prophesied for earthly gain, preached what was flattering to men's passions."[30]

How the Prophets Announced Their Message

Circumstances determined the manner by which the prophets made known their messages. Sometimes they uttered them aloud in public places. Sometimes they fixed their predictions to the gates of the Temple. Sometimes they walked publicly about in sack cloth and ashes and other external signs of sorrow and repentance to impress upon the people the need for repentance. Sometimes they used striking means to attain their purposes, e. g. Jeremias put bonds and yokes on his neck (Jer 27:2) to intimate the subjection that God would bring on the nation which Nabuchodonosor would subdue.

Some of the prophets spoke in the third person to emphasize the fact that they were speaking for God.

Classification of Prophets

The prophets in the period after Moses may be divided in the Earlier and the Later Prophets:

EARLIER PROPHETS (ORAL): i. e. those who only preached orally, and did not put their discourses into writing. Numbered in this group are Samuel, Gad, Nathan, Elias, and Eliseus.

LATER PROPHETS (LITERARY): i. e. those who not only preached but also wrote down their discourses and prophecies. This group is divided into the:

MAJOR PROPHETS—because of the great extent of their writing:

Isaias	Ezechiel
Jeremias	Daniel

MINOR PROPHETS:

Osee	Nahum
Joel	Habacuc
Amos	Sophonias
Abdias	Aggeus
Jonas	Zacharias
Micheas	Malachias

All the prophets exercised their ministry in the kingdom of Juda with the exception of Osee, Amos, and Jonas, who lived in the kingdom of Israel.

Isaias

"The book of Isaias surpasses all other prophetical books in the richness of its prophecies, the importance of the teachings, the power of its style, and the splendor of its poetry."[31]

Because of his description of Christ and Christ's work, Isaias is called the Evangelist of the O. T.

Isaias was the son of Amos. Since he had influence at court, we may infer that he was from an influential family. The date of his birth may be put about 770-760 B.C. He married a prophetess who bore him two sons. He exercised his ministry during the reign of kings Joathan, Achaz, and Ezechias. Tradition claims he died a martyr's death, but the date is unknown.

Contents: This book contains two parts—a book of judgements (1-35) and a book of consolations (40-66). In the first part Isaias describes the punishments which God will inflict upon the pagan nations and upon the chosen people; in the second part he predicts the liberation of the chosen people from the Babylonian captivity and foretells the establishment of the Messianic kingdom. In chapters 36 to 39 (the historical section) Isaias describes the invasion of Juda by the Assyrian Sennacherib.

Doctrine: Isaias stresses particularly the holiness and majesty of God. Before the supreme greatness of God, man is nothing; therefore pride should be humbled. God will have "His day" when He will punish the wicked and when His people will glorify Him. Isaias foretells the glorious coming of the Messiah and the work He is to do. (Cf. Appendix IV for some of his Messianic prophecies.)

Jeremias

Jeremias, a native of Anathoth, a village near Jerusalem, was a member of the priestly family who lived at the close of the seventh and the beginning of the sixth century B. C. He was called at an early age (during the thirteenth year of Josias' reign) to be a prophet, and he exercised his ministry until after the destruction of Jerusalem. He lived during the most tragic period of Jewish history, taking an active part in religious reform. His warnings were ignored and he incurred the hatred of his own countrymen. He dictated his prophecies to Baruch in 605 and 604 B. C. After having been faithful to the difficult mission he received from God, he died in Egypt.

Contents: This book contains two main divisions; chapters 1 to 45 contain "discourses threatening punishments which are aimed directly against Juda and are intermingled with narratives of personal and national events," and chaptres 46 to 51 consist of discourses "containing threats against nine heathen nations and intended to warn Juda indirectly against the polytheism and the policy of these people.'

Doctrine: The work of Jeremias is replete with the great themes of prophetical teaching: God is the Creator and

Ruler of the universe; He is just and merciful. Jeremias' continued calls to repentance and conversion are the antidotes to sin, particularly the sin of idolatry. He sketches the Messianic restoration which is to come.

Lamentations

"In the Greek and Latin Bibles, Lamentations forms an appendix to the Book of Jeremias and has a prologue which attributes them to the prophet. In the Hebrew Bible, however, they form a separate book, classed with the Hagiographa between Ruth and Ecclesiastes, and without either prologue or attribution to Jeremias."[32] Although some critics question the total or partial authorship of Jeremias, Catholic authors, on the whole, follow the traditional view, acknowledging Jeremias as the author.

Contents: This book of five chapters consists of as many short elegies which describe the destruction of Jerusalem and the suffering and the misery of its people. "Lamentations" presents a lesson on the justice of God, Who punished Jerusalem for its sins. However, God pardons and grants mercy; hence, we must hope in Him.

Baruch

This book was written by Baruch, Jeremias' secretary and apostle. He was from a noble family. After the fall of Jerusalem he was carried away with Jeremias to Egypt.

Contents: The first five chapters exhort the Jewish exiles to repentance and promise them a glorious release. The sixth chapter is an epistle of Jeremias, written just before the deportation of 586 B. C., warning those being led into Babylonian captivity against the idolatry which they will encounter.

E z e c h i e l

Ezechiel belonged to the priestly family. He was probably among those deported in 598-597 B. C. after the capture of Jerusalem. His wife died in the ninth year of the Exile. Some scholars think that he prophesied first in Palestine and later in Chaldea. He was called to be a prophet in the fifth year of the Exile (593/592 B.C.). The date of his last prophecy is 571/570. How long he lived after that is unknown.

Contents: This book of forty-eight chapters is divided into three parts: 1) chapters 1 to 24, with some exceptions, contain Ezechiel's dire prophecies concerning Jerusalem before its destruction in 586 B.C.; 2) chapters 25 to 32 contain prophecies against the nations: Ammon, Moab, the Philistines, Tyre and Sidon; 3) chapters 33 to 48 concern the national and religious restoration which is to come. These chapters are filled with hope and encouragement.

Doctrine: Ezechiel's teaching is similar to that of Isaias and Jeremias with this important addition: until this time, the exercise of divine justice was looked upon from a national aspect—the people were rewarded or punished as a whole. Ezechiel proclaims for the future the principle of individual retribution—individual reward and punishment.

Daniel

The book of Daniel presents many difficulties both as to its authorship and its contents. It was written in three languages; Hebrew, Aramaic, and Greek.

The authorship of this book is open to considerable debate. Some Catholic scholars offer the hypothesis that an inspired author of Machabean era considerably revised the book; others that an author of probably the second century B. C. wrote it, drawing upon documents which go back in date to Daniel's time. There are also other opinions.

Daniel, who according to Josephus belonged to the royal family of Sedecias, the last king of Juda, was led captive to Babylon by Nabuchodonosor in 605 B. C. His skill at interpreting dreams raised him to a very high position in the Babylonian empire.

Contents: This book, which consists of fourteen chapters, may be generally divided as follows: chapters 1 to 6 contain episodes in the life of Daniel; chapters 7 to 12 relate apocalyptic visions, narrated in the first person; chapters 13 and 14 contain the story of Susanna, a chaste Jewish woman, and the stories of Bel and the dragon.

Doctrine: The book of Daniel contains teaching which are almost entirely concerned with the Messianic future; it also contains teachings on God, His goodness, power, and providence.

The Twelve Minor Prophets

"The Twelve Minor Prophets, Osee, Joel, Amos, Abdias, Jonas, Micheas, Nahum, Habacuc, Sophonias, Aggeus, Zacharias, and Malachias already formed a collection by the time Ecclesiasticus was written, i. e. between 200 and 180 B. C. After having mentioned Isaias, Jeremias, and Ezechiel, the author speaks of the "Twelve Prophets" without naming them."[33] These books present a great variety of style and theme; and they furnish interesting information of social, political, and religious conditions.

1—OSEE was a native of the Northern Kingdom of Israel who exercised his prophetical ministry towards the end of the reign of Jeroboam III. He calls himself (1:1) the son of Bieri. He married Gomer by whom he had three children.

The fourteen chapters of this book offer the following: 1 to 3 explain in symbolic language the relations and covenant between God and Israel; in 4 to 9, Israel's sins are reproved and the coming punishment is foretold; in 10 to 14 the penalty is insisted on, but it will lead to their ultimate salvation.

2—JOEL, son of Pethuel, seems to have prophecied in Juda, probably in Jerusalem itself.

In the three chapters of this book, Joel describes the evils about to befall Juda and urges the people to repentance; he predicts the blessings of the Messianic kingdom, the outpouring of the Holy Spirit, and the judging of all nations.

3—AMOS, a shepherd and a cultivator of figs, was born in Thecua, near Bethlehem. He left Juda to carry out his prophetical mission in Israel during the reign of Jeroboam II (c. 760-750 B. C.).

The nine chapters of this book contain the following: 1) a prologue consisting of a series of prophecies against Israel's neighboring states and Israel itself; 2) further prophecies against Israel; 3) five visions interspersed with some addresses; 4) an epilogue describing the restoration of David's kingdom.

4—ABDIAS, about whom nothing is known, wrote the shortest book in the O. T. (1 chapter). The theme of the book is the destruction of Edom because of its iniquities, and the restoration of Israel.

5—JONAS was probably a contemporary of Jeroboam II and a member of the Northern Kingdom.

In chapters 1 and 2 Jonas' attempts to resist God's order that he go to preach in Ninive and the account of his being swallowed by a great fish are recorded. In chapters 3 and 4 the accomplishment of his mission and the repentance of Ninive are recounted.

Chapter 2:1—"JONAS WAS IN THE BELLY OF THE FISH, ETC." "It is not said either here or in the Gospels what kind of great fish it was that swallowed Jonas. Both the shark and sperm whale are found in the Mediterranean and are capable of swallowing a body bigger than a man's. The period of three days and three nights signifies in Hebrew usage a part of three days including the whole of the second; Cf. Est 4:16; 5:1; Mt 12:40. As Jonas prayed in the belly of the fish, 2:2, it does not seem possible to hold that he died and was restored to life."[34]

6—MICHEAS came from Maraseth, a village about thirty miles southwest of Jerusalem. He was a contemporary of Isaias, exercising his ministry during the reigns of Joatham, Achaz, and Ezechias.

The seven chapters of this book may be divided into three parts: 1 and 2 contain God's judgements against Israel and Juda; 3 to 5 contain a condemnation of the sins of the false prophets and judges; 6 and 7 contain a dialogue between God and Israel.

7—NAHUM, who was from Elkash, wrote a work of three chapters which contain poems on the power of God and the consolation of Israel, and which tell of the fate of Ninive.

8—HABACUC, about whom nothing is known, tells of the foreign conqueror and the problems which his victories and his presence raise, and it concludes with a prayer asking God to intervent in favor of His people.

9—SOPHONIAS, of royal descent (1:1), exercised his ministry under Josias, King of Juda (640-609 B. C.). His book of three chapters contains the threats of God's judgement; the call to repentance; the denunciation of Jerusalem, etc.; it ends with a note of encouragement and hope.

10—AGGEUS, in the three chapters that comprise his book, urges the people to rebuild the Temple, rebukes them for their indifference, and tells them that the Temple will be more glorious because the Messias will enter it.

11—ZACHARIAS seems to have belonged to a priestly family. The fourteen chapters of his book are a companion work to Aggeus. Among other things, the prophet encourages the rebuilding of the Temple, seeing in the completion of the

Temple the prelude to the new and glorious age of the Messias. This book contains details about the Passion of Christ.

12—MALACHIAS was the last prophet before John the Baptist. In the four chapters of his work, Malachias rebukes the priests for neglecting the worship of God and the teaching of the Law; he strikes at the abuses of mixed marriages and divorce; he predicts the coming of the Messias and His precursor (St. John the Baptist); he announces a new Sacrifice (1:11), i. e. the Mass.

PART III

THE NEW TESTAMENT

CHAPTER XI

THE JEWISH WORLD IN NEW TESTAMENT TIMES

T O understand adequately the historical books of the N.
T., it is necessary to have some knowledge of the political, social-economic, and religious conditions that prevailed
in the lives of the Jews who lived in N. T. times. In a short
work of this type only the essentials can be presented. More
detailed information can be obtained from the books recom-
mended in the Bibliography.

The Political Conditions of Palestine

Up to the fall of the Kingdom of Juda in 586 B. C., the
Hebrew religion and the Hebrew nation had been identi-
fied. When political independence was lost, the process began that would make Judaism a religion. In N. T. times
Judea was no longer an independent state, but a province of
a world empire; it had a much smaller area than when it
was ruled by the earlier Hebrew kings. The territory in
which the Jews formed a majority of the population was limited to Judea, Galilee, and Peraea—a region surrounded by
Gentile populations in the north, east, and south.

At the time of Christ's birth (c. 7 B. C.) Palestine was a
part of the Roman Empire and the country was united under

Herod the Great, who was the first king since Solomon to bring all Palestine under one rule. When he died in 4 B. C., Palestine was divided among his three sons: Archelaus received the title "king" and ruled Samaria, Judea, and northern Idumea; Herod Antipas ruled Galilee and Peraea; Philip governed Batania. To Salome, his sister, Herod the Great bequeathed the towns of Phasaelis, Archelais, Azotus, and Jamnia. Emperor Augustus approved this division, but he gave Archelaus the title ethnarch instead of king. After ten years of misrule Archelaus was deposed (A. D. 6) and a Roman procurator appointed in his place. The procurator was responsible to the Emperor, but dependent upon the Roman governor of Syria for military support. This accounts for Pilate being procurator at the time of Christ's passion.

The Sanhedrin. This consisted of a group of seventy-one members, including the high priest. By Christ's time it had lost much of its former power, but it still retained a considerable amount of authority over the Jewish people, particularly in Judea. It had its own police and could make arrests and inflict corporal punishment. While it could vote the death sentence, it seems most likely that it needed the ratification of the procurator.

Jews of the Diaspora. "The name Diaspora (from the Greek word meaning 'dispersion') was given to those Jewish communities which were settled outside Palestine. The dispersion of the Hebrews abroad began with the deportations of the conquered by the Assyrian and Babylonian rulers in the eighth, seventh, and sixth centuries B. C. Many of the early exiles lost their identity as Hebrews, and were absorbed by the population of the area where they dwelt. The Babylonian exiles, however, in large measure, retained their distinctive character, adhered to Jewish religious beliefs and practices, married their own and dwelt in Jewish communities. The number of Jews of the Diaspora is estimated in millions. Their language was Greek. The largest communities were found in the great cities, such as Antioch, Alexander, and Rome. The most notable important Jewish centre outside of Palestine was in Alexandria." [1]

Social and Economic Conditions in Palestine in N. T. Times

It is the opinion of some writers that Palestine was one of the most prosperous countries of the empire. It was principally an agricultural country. In addition to its principal crops of wheat and barley, it produced fruit in abundance. The forest of Palestine had not yet been destroyed so that timber was plentiful in comparison with modern times. The pasturing of sheep and goats no longer had the economic importance which it possessed in O. T. times. Trade and commerce were not carried on a large scale.

At the time of Christ, the population is estimated to have been about two million, including Transjordan.

There were no middle classes in N. T. times. The people were either very wealthy or very poor. Wealth came from commerce and property. The employments of the poor were agriculture, fishing, crafts, and unskilled labor. The first disciples of Christ were fishermen. Christ and St. Joseph were craftsmen (carpenters).

The land of the wealthy was tilled by the peasant who lived in the village and had his own strip of farm land in the neighborhood. After paying rent, taxes to Rome (twenty-five percent of the yield), and tithes for the Temple (twenty-two percent of the remainder), the average peasant had very little left.

Beneath the fishermen, craftsmen, and peasants were the unskilled laborers, the "hirelings" of the Gospel. Below these unskilled laborers were the social outcasts: the Samaritans (Jews of mixed origin), the tax collectors, the sick, crippled, aged, orphans, beggars, etc. Slavery was rare in Palestine.

Because of the general poverty that prevailed early marriages were the rule. A boy or girl of twelve years was regarded as grown enough to leave home; possibly the family wished to be rid of them as soon as possible.

The wealthy were able to buy the imported foods and clothes. The poor ate very simply, their staple food being wheat or barley bread and dried fish. Meat was a rare treat. The usual vegetables were leeks, lentils, and beans. Dried fruit and domestic wine completed the tables of the poor.

The poor man probably had no more than one set of garments: the tunic, and a cloak for inclement weather and for sleeping. The houses of the poor were of stone, one or two stories, usually shared by several families. The houses, even in the villages, were built very close together with only narrow alleys left for passage and for the disposal of refuse. The site of the village was determined by the availability of water. The water supply was supplemented by cisterns.

Religious Conditions of the Jews in N. T. Times

The Temple and the Priesthood. The Temple of Jerusalem was the official center of Jewish worship, and the only place where sacrifice could be legitimately offered. Every pious Jew, whether in Palestine or abroad, tried to visit the

Temple during one of the important annual feasts. This magnificent Temple was razed to the ground in A.D. 70 by the Romans, shortly after it was completed.

The Jewish priesthood was a distinct hereditary order which enjoyed a position of great importance. "Since the number of priests were far in excess of that necessary for the Temple service, they were divided into twenty-four courses, each of which served in turn. Within the courses there were further divisions into specialized offices which involved a difference in rank. The Levites, like the priests, were a hereditary order. They were intrusted with subordinate duties (singers, janitors, servants of the priests).

"The priests and the Temple services were maintained by revenues from the people. To the priests belonged the first-fruits and the first-born animals, and the money paid for the adoption of first-born sons; portions of sacrificial victims; tithes on all produce or profits; voluntary and votive offerings; and a half-shekel annual tax on every male Israelite over twenty years of age." [2]

The Synagogue. In N. T. times the synagogue was the place where the Jews gathered principally for religious instructions. The term was also used to signify the assembly of people. The synagogue as a religious institution originated during the Babylonian Exile, when the Jews had no Temple. After destruction of the Temple these synagogues took on a definite religious character in addition to being centers for the study of the Scriptures and the Law. The ruler of the synagogue was the most important official upon whom fell the duties of keeping order, determining who was to read the Scriptures or who was to address the congregation. Outsiders were sometimes invited to speak in these synagogues.

THE HISTORICAL BOOKS OF THE NEW TESTAMENT

CHAPTER XII

THE historical books of the N. T. are those which are concerned with the life and teaching of Christ and the early history of the Church. They are the Gospels of Matthew, Mark, Luke, and John, and the Acts of the Apostles.

The Gospel

The word "gospel" is derived from the Old English "godspell" which means "good news" and which is a translation of the Greek word "euangelion." In the N. T., the word denotes the good news of salvation proclaimed by Christ during His earthy life and transmitted to the world by the Apostles.

The written Gospel was preceded by the oral Gospel. Christ taught by word of mouth alone and for some years the Apostles followed His example. As the years passed and the number of Christ's original disciples became smaller, it was deemed necessary that what had been orally delivered concerning Christ and His teaching should be put in writing. From these writings the following have been placed on the list of sacred books: the Gospels of Matthew, Mark, Luke, and John.

The writers of these Gospels are called "Evangelists."

Symbols of the Evangelists

Since the time of St. Irenaeus (c. 130-202) each Evangelist has been assigned one of the four animals described by Ezechiel (1:5-10) and St. John in the Apocalypse (4:6): St. Matthew—a man; St. Mark—a lion; St. Luke—a steer and St. John—an eagle.

Gospel of Saint Matthew

"The First Gospel in rank is St. Matthew. We have early witness that it was regarded as the first to be written, and there is absolutely no ancient witness to the contrary. From the time we have any Christian writings, we find St. Matthew quoted more than any other Gospel." [3] This Gospel narrates the life of Christ—describing the infancy, the hidden life, the public life in Galilee, Judea, and Jerusalem, the Passion, Death, and Resurrection.

Matthew, son of Alpheus (Mk 2:14) and an Apostle of Christ, is the author of this Gospel. He was wealthy and educated. He is called "Levi" twice in the Gospels (Mk 2:14; Lk 5:27). After Pentecost Sunday he preached in Judea. Tradition adds that he preached the Gospel to the Gentiles, possibly in Ethiopia, Persia or Parthia. His feast is celebrated on September 21.

Matthew wrote his Gospel probably between A.D. 40-50. The common opinion of the Fathers is that the Gospel was written in Palestine.

Purpose of the Gospel. This Gospel was written in Aramaic for the Jews of Palestine to prove that Christ was the Messias foretold in the O. T., Who came to establish a new Kingdom of Heaven—the Church, and to show incredulous Jews that by their sins, their prejudices, and their rejection of the Messias they were excluded as a nation from the Messianic salvation to which the pagans were now called.

Brief Content Analysis. (The contents for the Gospels, Acts, Epistles, and Apocalypse will be taken primarily from the excellent little work: "Analysis of the New Testament," a Grail Publication, St. Meinrad, Indiana.).

Analysis: THE FIRST PART (1:1-4:11) by the narration of events which preceded and prepared for our Lord's public life, disposes the reader to acknowledge the Messias and willingly to receive His teaching. 1. The history of the infancy depicts Jesus as the Messias foretold by the prophets (1:1—2:23). 2. Jesus is depicted as the Messias in the proximate preparation for His Public life (3:1—4:11).

THE SECOND PART (4:12—14:12) proves from the Public Life that Jesus is the Messias and points out the cause of hatred on the part of Pharisees. 1. Jesus as teacher and legislator (5:1—7:29). In the sermon on the Mount, Jesus appears as the lawgiver who comes to perfect the Old Law. 2. Jesus as a wonder-worker (8:1—9:3). Miracles are narrated to show the fulfillment of prophecies, to attract souls to so merciful a Savior, and to expose the perversity of the Pharisees. 3. Jesus as the founder of a new kingdom (9:35—13:52), intimated in the call of the first four disciples (4:18-22).

THE THIRD PART (14:13—20:28) treats of the progress of the kingdom within the Apostles. 1. The Apostles acknowledge and profess the divinity of Christ as a preparation for their difficult office (14:13-36); two miracles effect this. 2. The Apostles must avoid the Pharisees and their perverse teachings (15:1–16:12). 3. The Apostles are placed under the primacy of Peter (16:13–17:26). 4. Jesus instructs His Apostles regarding their conduct as princes of the Church (18:1–20:28).

THE FOURTH PART (20:29–28:20) announces the complete rejection of the synagogue and the foundation of the Church. 1. As an introduction the evangelist narrates three symbolic facts, which serve to remove the "scandal of the cross" and to make manifest the guilt of the Jews (20:29–21:22). 2. Final encounter with the scribes and Pharisees which led to their rejection (21:23–23:39). 3. Escatological discourse; since the people and their leaders are rejected, Jesus instructs the Apostles alone concerning the judgment to come (24:1–25:46). 4. The history of the Passion and the Resurrection (26:1–28:15). The narrative clearly brings out the fault of the scribes and Pharisees and their voluntary blindness. 5. The mission of the Apostles to all nations (28:16-20).

Gospel of Saint Mark

This Gospel describes Christ's miracles and preaching in Galilee, His journey to Jerusalem, and His Passion, Death, and Resurrection.

Mark, the author of this Gospel, was probably born in Jerusalem, where his mother Mary owned a house (where it is probable that Christ instituted the Holy Eucharist and the Holy Ghost descended upon the Apostles). Peter probably baptized Mark whom he calls his son, i. e., his spiritual son (1 Pt 5:13). Mark accompanied Paul to Antioch (Act 12:25) and was his companion for a while on Paul's first missionary journey. Later he traveled with Barnabas to Cyprus (Act 15:39 f). Tradition ascribes to Mark the founding of the Church in Alexandria, where his body was venerated until the Venetians carried it to their own city. His feast is celebrated on April 25th.

Tradition tells us that Mark handed down to us in writing what had been preached by Peter. This Gospel was written in Rome sometimes between A. D. 55 and 62.

Purpose of the Gospel. St. Mark's purpose is to demonstrate to the Romans Christ's divinity. To prove this he records nineteen of Christ's miracles and shows His power over demons.

Brief Content Analysis: THE FIRST PART (1:21–9:28) describes how Christ, by His Galilean ministry, proved that He was the Son of God. 1. Our Lord's miracles at Capharnaum and His prophecies (1:21–2:12). 2. The effects produced by these first miracles on various classes of people (2:13–3:35). 3. He prepares His chosen disciples for their first mission; they are sent out (4:1–6:32). 4. During the last months of the Galilean ministry He manifests His divine power more clearly to the people and especially to His disciples (6:34–9:28).

THE SECOND PART (9:29–13:37) treats principally of doctrine by which Our Lord prepares His disciples for their future work. 1. The journey to Jerusalem (9:29–10:52). 2. The last days before the Passion; the first three days of Holy Week (11:1–13:37).

THE THIRD PART (14:1—16:20) treats of the Passion and the glory of Christ.

Gospel of Saint Luke

The Third Gospel contains an account of the infancy of Christ; His ministry in Galilee and His journey to Jerusalem, His Passion, Death and Resurrection.

Luke, the author of this Gospel, was a native of Antioch, a pagan by birth (Col 4:10-14), a physician (Col 4:14), and, according to tradition, a painter. He was one of the earliest converts to the Faith. He was Paul's missionary companion on part of the latter's second and third missionary journeys (Act 16:10—17:20: 5-21). Luke was with Paul during his imprisonment in Caesarea (Act 24:23). He went to Rome with Paul (Act 27:1-28) and was with him during his second imprisonment there (2 Tm 4:11). Little is known of his subsequent life. His feast is celebrated on October 18. Many characteristic features of this Gospel show the influence of Saint Paul.

Since references to the destruction of Jerusalem (A. D. 70) are in the future and there is no indication that the prophecy has been fulfilled, we may conclude that the Gospel was written before that event. Evidence points to its composition before A.D. 63.

The place of its composition is uncertain. Some authors held or hold for Achaia (Greece), Alexandria or Macedonia, Caesarea, Ephesus or Rome.

Purpose of the Gospel. Luke addressed his Gospel of

twenty-four chapters to the distinguished person, Theophilus. Indirectly, however, this Gospel was intended for Gentile converts. He was anxious to supply them with a deeper and more accurate knowledge of their faith, and to show them on what a firm basis their faith was founded.

Brief Content Analysis: THE FIRST PART (1:5—4:13) narrates the happenings which preceded the public ministry of our Lord. The narrative tends primarily to lead the Gentiles to acknowledge that Jesus Christ is the Son of God and secondarily to show the Jews that Jesus is the promised Messias. 1. History of the Infancy (1:5-2:52). 2. The proximate preparation of Jesus for the public exercise of His ministry (3:1-4:13).

THE SECOND PART (4:14-9:50) narrates the ministry of our Lord in Galilee. 1. Unsuccessful ministry in Nazareth (4:14-30. 2. By His miracles He excites the admiration of the people; His mercy towards sinners and the rejection of the pharisaical traditions draw upon Him the hatred of the Pharisees (4:31-6:11). 3. The beginnings of the new Messianic kingdom (6:12-49). 4. Jesus manifests His mercy to various classes to show that none who are properly disposed will be excluded from the new kingdom (7:1-50). 5. While passing through Galilee, He prepares the Apostles for their mission (8:1-9:6). 6. Returning from this mission, the faith of the Apostles is confirmed by new miracles; Christ prepares them for the announcement of His Passion (9:7-50).

THE THIRD PART (9:51—19:27) narrates our Lord's last journeys to Jerusalem and treats principally of doctrine. 1. The journey to the feast of tabernacles; Jesus instructs His disciples in the principles of the more perfect life (9:51-11:

54). 2. The journeys of our Lord from the feast of the purification to the feast of tabernacles; continued instruction (12:
1–13:9). 3. The journey through Perea; the errors of the
Pharisees; the call of the Gentiles (13:10–17:10). 4. The last
of the Gentiles (17:11–19:27).

THE FOURTH PART (19:29-24:53) treats of the Passion
and the glorification of Christ. 1. Preparation for the Passion (19:29-22:38). 2. The Passion of our Savior (22:39-23-
:56). In the history of the Passion, St. Luke clearly points
out the guilt of the entire people and the innocence of Jesus.
Neither Herod (not mentioned by the other Evangelists)
nor Pilate find any fault in Him. True to his purpose, St.
Luke calls attention to the mercy of our Savior. Christ prays
for His persecutors and promises paradise to the repentant
thief. 3. The glorification of Christ (24:1-53).

Gospel of Saint John

"In taking up the Gospel according to Saint John, the
reader will notice at once a difference from the viewpoint
of the Synoptics i. e., the first three Gospels. The first three
Evangelists move among the plain realities and the simpler
folk of Galilee. The fourth strikes a higher note in his account of our Lord's life and teachings. The public life of
Jesus is given chiefly as it touches Jerusalem. For the Synoptics the ministry in Galilee is the chief concern. This field
John seldom invades, and when he does it is with his own
purpose in view. He adds, however, many details throughout the Gospel which are passed over by the others." [4]

St. John the Apostle, also called the Evangelist and the Beloved Disciple of Jesus, is the author of the Fourth Gospel.

He was the son of Zebedee (Mk 1:20), a prosperous fisherman of Bethsaida on Lake Tiberias. John's brother was also an Apostle, James the Greater. John was influenced by St. John the Baptist to follow Christ. He went with Christ to Galilee where he attended the wedding feast at Cana and witnessed Christ's first public miracle (Jn 2:1-12). He returned to his fishing until called by Christ to be His Apostle. John was Christ's favorite who received many special favors. He witnessed the restoration to life of Jairus' daughter (Mk 5:37; Lk 8:51); the Transfiguration (Mt 17:1-8; Mk 9:1-7; Lk 9:28-36); the cure of Peter's mother-in-law (Mk 1:29). Together with Peter, he was commissioned by Christ to prepare for the Last Supper (Lk 22:8), during which he reclined beside the Master (Lk 13:23). He witnessed Christ's agony in the Garden of Gethsemani (Mt 26:37; Mk 14:33), and he was intrusted with the care of Mary by the dying Christ (Jn 19:26 f). After the descent of the Holy Ghost, Peter and John labored in Jerusalem (Act 3:1 f) and Samaria (Act 8:14 f). Towards the end of his life he was banished to Patmos because of his teaching (Ap 1:9), probably during the reign of Domitian (A. D. 81-96). According to tradition, John was the only Apostle to die a natural death. His feast is celebrated on December 26. This Gospel was probably written before A.D. 100 at Ephesus.

Purpose of the Gospel. John's purpose was to show that Jesus is the Son of God. He proves his point by recounting appropriate miracles and words.

Brief Content Analysis: THE FIRST PART (1:9—12:50) records the manifestation of the divinity of Jesus in His public works and teaching. 1. Jesus is received with more or less perfect faith in Judea, Galilee and Samaris (1:19-4:54). 2. the divinity of Jesus is assailed and rejected by the Pharisees (5:1-11:56). 3. The heavenly Father wishes to manifest the glory of Christ before the plans of the Pharisees are carried out. Jesus' triumph prefigures the triumph of His Resurrection (12:1-50).

THE SECOND PART (13:1-17:26) contains a manifestation of the divinity of Christ in His Passion, Death and Resurrection. 1. This manifestation is received with faith by the disciples at the Last Supper. 2. Manifestation of the divinity of Christ in His Passion and Death as assailed by His enemies (18:1-19:37). 3. Manifestation of the divinity of Christ in His triumph over His adversaries.

Acts of the Apostles

This book is an account or history of the earliest days of the Church, covering about thirty-five years from the Ascension of Christ to the close of St. Paul's first Roman imprisonment in about A. D. 63. It recounts some of the missionary activities of Peter and Paul, with allusions to James the Greater, John, James the Less, and certain disciples.

St. Luke, author of the Third Gospel, wrote this book probably in Rome. It was probably completed about A. D. 63.

Purpose of the Book. "Luke's purpose was to show Theophilus and the Christians that the Church of Christ was established by God for all men (Act 1:8). A secondary purpose may have been to vindicate Paul during his trial in Rome by showing how well he had been treated by the Romans on every occasion when the Jews had made accusations against him (Act 13:7-12; 16: 37-40, etc.)." [5]

Brief Content Analysis: THE FIRST PART (1:1–9:43). The origin of the Church and its propagation among the Jews. 1. Foundation of the universal Church and its beginnings among the Jews (1:1-2:47). 2. Propagation and confirmation of the Church among the Jews of Jerusalem (3:1-7:59). 3. The propagation of the Church among the Jews throughout Palestine and Syria (8:1-9:43).

THE SECOND PART (10:1-21:16). The Church, founded among the Gentiles by the First Apostles, is propagated by Paul. 1. The origin of the Church among the Gentiles and their charity for the Jewish converts (10:1-12:25). 2. Propagation of the Gospel among the Gentiles of Cyprus and southern Asia Minor. Settlement of the dispute concerning the observance of the Law (13:1-15:35). 3. Propagation of the Gospel among the Gentiles of Macedonia, Achia and the provinces of Asia (15:36-21:16).

THE THIRD PART (21:17-28:31) narrates the captivity of Paul and his appeal to Rome, where he bears witness to Christ. 1. Paul's captivity in Jerusalem (21:17-23:35). 2. Paul's captivity in Caesarea (24:1-26:32). 3. Paul's Journey to Rome; his imprisonment there (27:1-13).

CHAPTER XIII

THE EARLY AND PUBLIC LIFE OF CHRIST

O F necessity, this life of Christ will be brief, almost sketchy. Further knowledge of Christ may be obtained from the many lives which have been written about Him, some of which are contained in the Bibliography of this work. However, no matter how learned and detailed these works may be, none of them can compare with the simplicity and beauty of the original lives of Christ, the Holy Gospels. We earnestly entreat the reader to read these Gospels before any other life of Christ.

Christ's Early Life

THE ANNUNCIATION OF THE SAVIOUR (Lk 1:26-38). In Nazareth, a negligible little village of Galilee, which is about eighty-eight miles north of Jerusalem, there lived a "virgin betrothed to a man named Joseph, of the house of David, and the virgin's name was Mary" (27). Mary, also, belonged to the house of David; therefore, she and Joseph had the royal blood of David in their veins.

Among the Jews, legal marriage consisted of two stages:

the betrothal and the wedding itself. The former was more than a promise to marry; it was a perfectly legal marriage contract, the persons being husband and wife. After the betrothal, the parties continued to live apart with his or her respective family—a year if the bride was a virgin and a month if she were a widow. This time was spent in preparing the new home and its furnishings. After the necessary time had elapsed, the wedding itself took place, consisting of the bride's formal reception into her husband's home.

According to the custom of the time, Mary was probably thirteen or fourteen years of age and Joseph between the ages of eighteen and around forty at the time of their betrothal.

When the Angel Gabriel assured Mary that she would remain a virgin through the miraculous intervention of the Holy Spirit, she was willing to accept the sublime dignity of being the mother of the Messias.

Joseph noticed that Mary was with child "but being a just man, and not wishing to expose her to reproach, was minded to put her away privately." (i.e., break the betrothal without publicity). The doubts which Joseph experienced were dispelled in a divinely-inspired dream. (Mt. 1:18-25).

THE BIRTH OF JESUS (Lk 2:1-7; 2:8-20). When Rome decreed a census of all its people, Mary and Joseph had to go to Bethlehem to register, since Joseph and his family belonged to the house of David which originated in Bethlehem. Bethlehem was a very humble little town situated about six miles south of Jerusalem.

From Nazareth to Bethlehem is a distance of a little less than ninety-five miles. It probably took Mary and Joseph three or four days to make the trip by caravan.

While it is true that the inns of Bethlehem were crowded to capacity, nevertheless, room probably could have been made for Mary and Joseph. However, since there was so little privacy in these inns, the holy couple did not consider it a fitting place for the birth of the Saviour.

The place of Christ's birth was a stable, a grotto or small cave cut in the side of one of the little hills near the village. In Palestine, caves were frequently used as stables and even dwellings. "And she brought forth her first-born son, and wrapped him in swaddling clothes, and laid him in a manger." (2:7). The phrase "swaddling clothes" does not mean a lack of clothing, but the long, narrow bands of cloth wrapped around a new-born baby. The use of the term "manger" in the text implies a stable.

The term "first-born" does not mean that other children followed. This term merely indicates that no other children preceded Christ "The Evangelist wishes merely to stress the fact that the Mosaic Law of the first-born, involving various duties and privileges (Cf Ex 13:2) applied to Jesus also". [6] The Catholic Church has always taught that Mary was a virgin before, during, and after the birth of Christ.

The first to know of the birth of Christ were poor ignorant shepherds to whom an angel announced the glad tidings. These men visited the Infant Saviour and, on leaving, told others what they had witnessed.

THE CIRCUMCISION (Mk 1:25; Lk 2:21) AND THE PRESENTATION (Lk 2:22-38). Eight days after Christ's birth, He was circumcised and called Jesus. By the rite of circumcision a male child was initiated into the Jewish religion. It did not have to be performed by the priests; it could be done by the father of the child, or by others. The Holy Family probably moved to one of the houses in the village where the Infant Saviour was circumcised.

"According to Hebrew Law, a woman, after childbirth, was to be considered unclean and must keep to herself for forty days, if her child was a boy, eighty days if it was a girl. Then she was to present herself in theTemple for purification and make an offering, which, for the poor, was fixed at a pair of doves or pigeons. If the child was her first and a male, then according to the Law, he belonged to Yahweh like the firstlings of the flock and the first fruits of the field. Hence his parents were to buy him back by paying five shekels to the Temple. It was not necessary to bring the child to the Temple to present him to God, but the mother usually did so to invoke upon him the blessings of heaven."[7]

THE MAGI ADORE JESUS (Mt 2:1-12). The Magi (wise men) were originallya Median priestly tribe of clairvoyants. The term later was applied to astrologers, sorcerers, etc., of all nationalities. Since Matthew does not use the term in a derogatory sense, we may consider them as sages or wise men. They probably came from beyond the Jordan and the Red Sea, i. e., Nabatean Arabia. The nature of their gifts seems to confirm this, since Arabia was renowned for its gold, incense, and myrrh, the latter being an aromatic gum resin and costly perfume made from several shrubs and trees.

These Magi must have been aware of the Jewish expectation of the Messias.

The majority of Catholic biblical scholars consider the star which guided the Magi a special creation.

Matthew does not mention the number of the Magi, but the number is taken to be three because of the number of their gifts. Their names—Gaspar, Melchior and Balthasar, are only a medieval conjecture.

"Certainly the Presentation of the Child Jesus took place prior to the coming of the Magi. Saint Joseph would not have presumed to carry the Child to Jerusalem if Herod had been there seeking His life. The flight of the Holy Family into Egypt immediately after the departure of the Magi from Bethlehem (Mt 2:13) would also indicate this. It is very probable that the Child Jesus was at least a year old when the Magi came to Bethlehem." [8]

When the Magi reached Jerusalem they inquired of Herod the whereabouts of the Child, "the newly born king of the Jews." (2:2). That aged tyrant, who had murdered two of his sons on the mere suspicion of conspiracy, and was about to murder a third, feared for his throne. He told the Magi that when they found the Child they were to acquaint Him with His whereabouts so that he too might worship Him. This was not his intention at all; he was anxious to do away with this so-called "danger to his throne." The Magi found the Infant but they did not return to Herod because they were warned against this in a dream.

THE FLIGHT INTO EGYPT. MASSACRE OF THE INNOCENTS (Mt 2:13-18). Herod, enraged at the turn of events, ordered the slaughter of all male children under two years of age in Bethlehem and the surrounding territory. "He based the age limit on what the Magi had told him concerning the apparition of the star, allowing a generous margin in order to be sure that this time the Child would not escape him."[9]

Joseph was warned in a dream of the impending danger and ordered to flee into Egypt with Jesus and Mary. This he did. "Five or six days traveling would take the Holy Family to the frontier of Egypt, now an imperial Prefecture with a Jewish population of about one million, concentrated especially in Alexandria and Heliopolis." [10] Many Palestinian Jews took refuge in Egypt.

The number of male children slain by order of Herod is estimated to have been between twenty and thirty.

THE HOLY FAMILY AT NAZARETH (Mt 2:22-33; Lk 2:39-40). When Herod died, an angel appeared in a dream to Joseph telling him of this and instructing him to take Jesus and Mary back to the "land of Israel." If Joseph had intended to settle in Bethlehem, he soon changed his mind when he learned that Herod's son, Archelaus, a man of evil reputation, was now governing Judea. He decided to settle in Nazareth, Galilee, where Antipas ruled.

The Child Jesus was about two years of age when the Holy Family began to live in Nazareth. Except for a brief account of Christ's visit to the Temple, very little is known about the first thirty years or so of His life, often called His "hidden life." Luke tells us that "the child grew and became strong. He was full of wisdom and the grace of God was upon him" (2:40) and "Jesus advanced in wisdom and age and grace before God and men." (2:52).

For a brief account of the Hebrew home, food, clothing, etc., Chapter XI may be consulted. We can only surmise the peace and happiness that filled the home of the Holy Family, with Jesus helping His foster-father, Joseph, in the carpenter shop and Mary lovingly cleaning, cooking, serving and caring for her two loved ones.

Christ's daily language was Aramaic, spoken with an accent peculiar to the Galileans. "Since His country was near the border territory in which there was continual con-

tact with the surrounding Greek population, a certain knowledge of Greek was almost a necessary requirement. Hence it
is probable that he used Greek sometimes and even more
probable that He used Hebrew." [11]

Jesus had no brothers or sisters, Mary being a virgin before, during, and after the birth of Christ. He did have relatives, cousins who were called "brothers" and "sisters" according to Hebrew usage.

THE CHILD JESUS IN THE TEMPLE (Lk. 15:41-50). Male
Jews living in Palestine were obliged to visit the Temple in
Jerusalem three times a year (Ex 23:17; 34:23) at the three
great feasts of the Pasch, Pentecost, and Tabernacles (Dt 16:
16). Children, including boys before their thirteenth year,
and women were not obliged to go. However, as would be
expected, many men took their families with them. Joseph
took Jesus and Mary on this occasion.

Those who had to travel from distant places like Nazareth usually made the journey with groups of relatives and
friends.

During the first evening of the return journey, when
families gathered together for evening rest, Jesus could not
be found. His parents, after unsuccessfully looking for Him
among relatives and friends, returned to Jerusalem, where
after three days they found Him in the Temple "sitting in the
midst of the teachers" (15:46). "And all who were listening
to Him were amazed at His understanding and His answers."
(15:47).

Christ's Public Life

The bulk of the Gospels is concerned with Christ's public life. In a work of this kind we can consider only those popular difficulties which require some explanation. The reader will find the books treating of Christ's public life in the Bibliography of this book.

The exact year of the beginning of Christ's public life is uncertain. However, when all available evidence is sifted and examined we might give A. D. 27-28 as the first year of Christ's public ministry.

We have no certain knowledge as to Christ's age when He began His public ministry. St. Luke's expression "about thirty years of age" (3:23) is elastic. Today this might mean one or two years more or less so that a man "about thirty" may be thirty-two or twenty-eight. To the ancient Jews this expression must have implied even greater leeway—judging from various indications. Hence, such an expression would allow for the addition of three or four units to the given number, so that a man at thirty-four might still be "about thirty."

The length of Christ's public life is likewise uncertain. Ricciotti holds for a public life of about two and a half years, placing Christ's age at the time of His death at thirty-four and a half or thirty-five and a half years old.

Hartdegen would seem to favor a two-year public life placing Christ's death in A. D. 30. According to his chronological order Christ would have been about thirty-five and a half years old at the time of His death.[12]

Steinmueller-Sullivan tell us that "on the basis of Scriptural (John 8:57) and patristic evidence (Irenaeus, Adv.

Haer 2, 22, 5) that Christ during some phase of His public life was in His forties, it seems very probable that He was born about 8 B. C., began His public ministry A. D. 29 or 30, and died three years later." [13]

In *A Catholic Commentary on Holy Scripture,* we find that Christ began His public ministry about A. D. 29 and was crucified April 3, A.D. 33.[14]

"If we accept the end of A. U. C. 746 (8 B. C.) for the date of the Nativity, and April 786 A. U. C. (A. D. 33) for that of the Crucifixion, our Lord would have been in His fortieth year at the time of His death."[15]

This writer presents these different opinions to demonstrate that this particular aspect of Christ's life is still undecided.

THE BAPTISM OF CHRIST (Mt 3:13-17; Mk 1:9-11; Lk 3:21-22). The baptism which John administered to Christ was not the Sacramental one, but a baptism of repentance for the forgiveness of sin (Lk 3:3). It was a symbol of internal holiness and its reception demanded internal reform. Christ did not have to undergo this ceremony, but He insisted upon it so as to carry out the will of His Heavenly Father, whereby His public mission would be solemnly inaugurated by this public act of humility during which He was to be proclaimed the beloved Son of God.

Immediately after the ceremony, the Holy Spirit, in the visible form of a dove, descended upon Him and the voice of God the Father was heard speaking of His Beloved Son. Here we have the three Persons of the Holy Trinity clearly indicated.

THE TEMPTATION OF JESUS (Mt 4:1-11; Mk 1:12-13; Lk

4:1-13). After His baptism Jesus was impelled by the Spirit to withdraw into the desert so that He might prepare for His ministry. Christ's fast was one without food and drink for forty days and nights. It would seem that the devil appeared in bodily form and that the temptations were presented externally and were not merely an internal suggestion. However, the final temptation was probably a vision of all the kingdoms of the world, and was made directly to the mind of Christ.

"By reason of the hypostatic union our Lord was incapable of sin, nor, being without original sin, could He be tempted from within by concupiscence (i. e., by the inordinate desire consequent upon original sin). He could be tempted therefore, not by the lower nature itself, but only by the exterior suggestion of the Enemy." [16]

Christ submitted to temptation so that He might be like us in all things except sin (Heb. 2:17), to repair the harm done by the failure of Adam to resist the devil (Rom 5:14), to help us by His example (Heb 2:18; Heb 4:15).

CHRIST'S FIRST MIRACLE (Jn 2:1-11). Cana was a village in lower Galilee, about six miles northeast of Nazareth; it is probably the modern Kefr Kenna. "If, as is likely, Mary was present as a relative, the invitation to Jesus and His disciples would have been on her account, although Nathaniel may have had something to do with it. (He came from Cana). St. Joseph evidently was dead." [17]

Since nuptial festivities lasted a week, the exhaustion of the wine can be readily explained.

The verse: "What wouldst thou have me do, woman? My hour has not yet come" (4) is the cause of considerable discussion.

"There is, of course, no severity or disrespect in the address: 'Woman'; it is a respectful, if somewhat solemn, form of address in the Greek as well as in the Hebrew. For the rest of that first sentence, we must look to the language in which Christ spoke, the Aramaic, and then recognize that His words were: "Woman, never mind"; i.e., it is not for us to intervene here. Without disrespect, without brusqueness, the words are still a refusal; and for the reason stated. He had not intended to appear so before men until John the Baptist had finished his mission." [18]

SERMON ON THE MOUNT (Mt Chapters 5, 6, 7; Lk 6:20-49). This was a long discourse made by Christ during the early part of His public life. The place of its delivery is not certain; on a slope with a surrounding plain probably a few miles from Capharnaum. The Sermon is a compendium of the moral norms of Christianity. It contains the eight Beatitudes, calls the disciples the "salt of the earth," shows that the New Law is a completion and perfection of the Old Law, condemns religious hypocrisy, and contains instructions on prayer and the "Our Father."

It is not within the scope of this chapter to present an extensive consideration of Christ's public life. The several phases considered were chosen because they would seem to be the more popular aspects of His public life which have caused some difficulty. To say that these few aspects exhaust all the difficulties, major or minor, would be far from the truth.

In Chapter XV a brief consideration of Christ's miracles and parables will be offered.

CHAPTER XIV

THE PASSION AND DEATH OF CHRIST

THE LAST SUPPER (Mt 26:17-35; Mk 14:12-31; Lk 22:7-38; Jn 31:1 to 17:26). The feast of the Unleavened Bread is another name for the feast of the Passover (Cf. Ch. VI).

The "certain man" at whose home the Passover was to be celebrated was probably a very dear friend of Christ, possibly the father or other relative of Mark whose house, after Christ's death, became the habitual meeting place of the Christians of Jerusalem.

The usual Paschal ceremony was undoubtedly observed at the Last Supper, with the four cups of ritual wine, the unleavened bread, the wild herbs, and the roast lamb.

The four cups of wine played an important part in the ceremony, as follows:—"*First cup:* The head of the family pronounced a blessing over the wine, tasted it and passed the cup along for the others to drink of. The bitter herbs were then dipped into the common dish of thick sauce called Charoseth, and eaten; the same was done with the unleavened bread. Finally, the roast lamb was brought on. *Second cup:* The head of the family explained the symbolic significance of the meal, recalling again the miraculous deliverance of their forefathers from the bondage of Egypt The first part of the Hallel (Pss 112-113: 8) was then sung, and the second cup of wine taken. *Third cup:* the lamb was blessed and eaten, and the third cup of wine consumed. This was called the cup of benediction. *Fourth cup:* There followed the chanting of further psalms (Pss 113:8-117). A fourth cup of wine was then served, and after singing a hymn the guests departed. *It is generally believed that this became the new paschal supper of Christ's Body and Blood."* [19]

Many ancient and modern exegetes are of the opinion that Judas left the Upper Room before the Eucharist had been instituted.

THE AGONY IN THE GARDEN OF GETHSEMANI (Mt 26:30, 36-56; Mk 14:26, 32-52; Lk 22:39, 40-53; Jn 18:1-12). When Christ asked His Heavenly Father to remove the "cup," i.e., the lot that was befalling Him, He did not because He doubted the love, power, or will of the Father, but because as man He dreaded the impending suffering and death.

Luke mentions (22:44) that Christ's sweat became as blood. This "sweating of blood," known to physiologists as hematidrosis, has been recorded in the annals of medicine, being brought on by extremes of pain and mental anguish.

THE ARREST OF CHRIST (Mt 26:47-56; Mk 14:43-52; Lk 22:47-53; Jn 18:2-12). While Jesus was praying and suffering in the Garden at the foot of the Mount of Olives, Judas was completing his arrangement with the Jews, for the betrayal of Christ. (Mt 26:14-16; Mk 14:10f; Lk 22:3-6). The sum of thirty pieces of silver was paid to Judas for Christ's betrayal. The sum was a natural one for the Jewish priests to choose because the Law of the Jews laid it down as a price for a human person—a slave (Ex 21:32). In American money, Judas' reward for the betrayal would have been about $15.00.

In the Orient the kiss is a customary sign of respect; pupils kiss the hands of their teachers; friends kiss each other on the cheek. When Judas approached with an armed crowd of Roman soldiers and Jewish guards, he went up to Christ and kissed Him. This was the prearranged signal whereby the guards would know who was to be apprehended.

As if to show that He could free Himself if He so desired, Christ revealed His Divine power when He caused the arresting band to fall to the ground. With perfect freedom, Christ allowed Himself to be arrested after He tenderly prevented the arrest of His disciples. Overwhelmed by fear, the disciples, including an unclad youth (perhaps John Mark), fled from the scene.

THE RELIGIOUS TRIAL (Mt 26:57-27:1; Mk 14:53-15:1; Lk 22; 54-71; Jn 18:13-27). Shortly after midnight, Christ was brought before Annas, former high-priest, one of the most powerful men in Jerusalem and father-in-law of Caiphas, the then presiding high-priest. After unofficially asking questions about Christ's disciples and doctrines, Annas sent Christ to Caiphas, not before, however, one of his over-eager servants gave Christ a blow across the face.

Meanwhile, members of the Sanhedrin were secretly gathered to collect evidence against Jesus on a religious charge which would enable them to condemn Him to death. The examination of witnesses proved nothing. When Caiphas adjured the silent Christ to declare whether He was the Messias, the Son of God, Christ said that He was. The Sanhedrin then declared He had blasphemed and was worthy of death. The verdict had to be confirmed by Pilate, who, as Roman procurator, alone in Jerusalem held the right to pass sentence of death.

PETER'S DENIALS (Mt 26:69-75; Mk 14:66-72; Lk 22: 55-62; Jn 18:15-18, 25-27). Peter denied Christ three times as Christ had foretold. After the third denial a cock crowed, as was foretold, and when Jesus looked at Peter, the latter wept bitterly in sorrow for his horrible denial.

THE CIVIL TRIAL (Mt 27:2-26; Mk 15:1-15; Lk 23:1-25; Jn 18:28-19:16). The Sanhedrists feared that Pilate would not sanction a death sentence pronounced on purely religious grounds and arrived at through illegal methods. Hence they did not ask for a confirmation of their sentence, but referred the accused to his court for a new trial. Pilate refused the case on the grounds that it was within their jurisdiction. The Sanhedrists then changed the charges to political ones: Christ was a revolutionary leader who plotted to be king. Pilate, on examining Jesus, and finding that His kingdom was of a spiritual nature, returned to the Jews who remained outside the praetorium (lest they be defiled on the feast) and declared that he found Christ innocent. The Jews still clamored. To placate them Pilate sent Christ to Herod Antipas who had come to Jerusalem for the Pasch.

Christ remained silent before Herod, who sent Him back to Pilate robed in the white robe of a fool. By this action, Herod indicated that he, too, found no reason to condemn Jesus.

Pilate's examination of Christ had proved the charges against Him false. His wife sent him a message warning him not to become involved in the case.

Too weak to free Jesus, too fearful to condemn Him, Pilate tried to compromise by reminding the Jews it was their privilege during the Passover to ask for the release of any criminal. They were asked to choose between Christ and Barabbas, a notorious robber and murderer. When they chose the latter, Pilate sought to satisfy them by ordering Christ to be scourged.

THE SCOURGING AND CROWNING WITH THORNS (Mt 27: 26-30; Mk 15:15-19; Jn 19:1-3). Among the Romans flagellation generally preceded crucifixion. Sometimes it was a substitution for capital punishment or a means of extorting confessions. The condemned man was stripped of his clothing and bound to a column, probably with his hands above his head.

Roman citizens were usually scourged with rods. For the other form of scourging a distinctly Roman instrument was used—the flagellum. This instrument had a short handle to which were attached long, thick thongs, usually two of them. Balls of lead or the ankle-bones of sheep were placed a little distance away from the end of the thong. These thongs would cut the skin and the balls or little bones would make deep wounds into it.

According to Hebrew law, the number of strokes were limited to forty. The Romans imposed no limitations, but the victim had to survive so as to be able to carry his cross and die on it.

From the above explanation we can partly understand the horrible torments Christ suffered from the scourging.

After the terrible scourging, the Roman soldiers placed a purple cloak about His shoulders, a crown of thorns on His head, and a reed for a scepter in His hand. Christ was mocked as "King of the Jews." "And they kept striking Him on the head with a reed, and spitting upon Him, and bending their knees, they did homage to Him." (Mk 15:19).

When Pilate brought the pitiable Christ before the people, thinking that they might be moved to release Him, they, instigated by the priests, clamored for His crucifixion. Pilate then handed Christ over to be crucified, not before, however, he symbolically washed his hands—a Jewish rite signifying that one disclaimed all personal responsibility for an act. (Cf. Dt 21:1-9).

DESPAIR AND SUICIDE OF JUDAS (Mt 27:3-10; Act 1:15-20). We might mention here Judas' reaction after his despicable deed. Appearing before the chief priests and elders he confessed, "I have sinned in betraying innocent blood." (Mt 27:4) He received no satisfaction from them. Flinging the silver into the temple, he gave way to despair and hanged himself. With the money the chief priests bought the potter's field as a burial place for strangers.

THE WAY OF THE CROSS (Mt 27: 31-33; Mk 15:20-22; Lk 23:26-32; Jn 19:16-17). The Way of the Cross began at the praetorium (the residence or palace of the Procurator, Pilate) in the Fortress of Antonia at the northwest area of the temple and continued in a more or less east-west direction for about three-fifths of a mile to the hill of Golgotha.

Christ carried His own cross. "The shape of the cross is not certainly known. The X, Y, and T forms were in use, but in Our Lord's case the T-shape with upward prolongation of the vertical is witnessed by the best authority, (Irenaeus, Adv. Haer. 2, 24, 4) and leaves room for an inscription over His head. The transverse beam was called the patibulum and, in Rome at least, it was customary for the criminal to carry only this beam. This may be true of Our Lord."[20]

So weakened was Christ that it was necessary to have a certain Simon of Cyrene help Him to carry the cross. During the sorrowful journey Christ spoke to a group of sympathetic women who approached Him.

CRUCIFIXION AND DEATH (Mt 27:34-56; Mk 15:23-41; Lk 23:33-49; Jn 19:18-30). Golgotha, the place of execution, was a small hill outside the city walls which resembled a skull. (The name itself, "golgotha," is the local Aramaic word for skull.)

When Christ arrived at Calvary, He refused the wine mixed with narcotic myrrh. This potion was given to the condemned to help deaden pain. Together with the two thieves, Christ was stripped of His garments. His outer garments were divided into four parts, one for each of the soldiers assigned for the execution. Rather than divide the seamless inner garment, the soldiers cast lots to see whose it would be.

Christ was stretched on the ground and His hands were then nailed to the cross He had been carrying. If Christ carried the patibulum (the transverse beam) He was nailed to it and then raised to the standing vertical beam which would have had a notch cut into it to receive the patibulum. Christ's feet were then nailed to the cross.

Above His head was placed the title dictated by Pilate (written in Greek, Latin, and Hebrew): "Jesus of Nazareth, the King of the Jews." "The chief priests readily understood the shameful reproach to themselves implied in the title on the cross. They petitioned Pilate to change it to:

'He said, I am the King of the Jews.' Pilate refused. Thus the inscription on the cross of Christ became ironically a title of condemnation for a people who wilfully rejected their King and God."[21]

While Christ shed His Precious Blood, the Jews and the soldiers mocked and ridiculed Him. From noon until three o'clock, the hours in which Christ was on the cross, nature exhibited strange signs: there was darkness in Jerusalem at his death; the earth quaked; rocks were split; the veil of the temple was torn in two; tombs were opened and a number of persons who had died before this time rose and walked about.

The centurion and the soldiers acknowledged that Christ was indeed the Son of God and a just man.

It was customary to hasten the death of a crucified man by breaking his legs. When it came time to do so to Jesus, the soldiers found Christ already dead, so, instead, His side was pierced and immediately blood and water issued from it.

Christ died at three o'clock in the afternoon. Pilate was surprised to know that Christ had expired so soon. Christ's terrible preliminary tortures and suffering hastened His death.

THE LAST WORDS OF CHRIST. 1. "Father, forgive them, for they do not know what they are doing" (Lk 23:34). "The ignorance of the Jewish leaders was unquestionably culpable. They were fully responsible for the prejudice and deliberate blindness which caused them to mistake Christ for an imposter. Nonetheless, the Savior 'loved even His enemies and prayed for them who persecuted and calumniated Him'."[22]

2. "Amen I say to thee, this day thou shalt be with Me in paradise" (Lk 23:43). Christ addressed these words to the repentent thief who asked Him to remember him when He would come into His kingdom.

3. "Woman, behold thy son... Behold thy mother" (Jn 19:26-27). Jesus spoke the first words to His mother who stood at the foot of the cross together with Mary of Cleophas, Mary Magdalen, and St. John, the Beloved Disciple. The second part was spoken to St. John. "According to theologians St. John represented all mankind in receiving from the dying Savior the precious legacy of His mother. Here is realized that spiritual motherhood of Mary towards all the generations of men that are to come after John."[23]

4. "Eloi, Eloi, lama sabacthani?" are the Aramaic words for "My God, my God, why has thou forsaken me?" (Mk 15:34). "The fourth word was not, as is frequently thought, the cry of a soul utterly abandoned by God, but rather the beginning of the messianic psalm (Ps 21) which describes Christ's sufferings at length, His prayer for divine assistance, and His prophecy of liberation and victory over death."[24] "The desolation felt in the human soul of Christ is given expression in the Psalmist's words. But there is no question of despair or of abandonment of the humanity by the divinity. Christ was abandoned by God only in the sense that God did not spare Him the sufferings of the Passion and Crucifixion, but allowed His enemies to work their evil on Him."[25]

5. "I thirst" (Jn 19:28). The soldiers dipped a sponge into a sour wine—a mixture of sour wine and water called "posca"—and held it to Christ's mouth by means of a reed or cane.

6. "It is consummated" (Jn 19:30). By these words,

Christ meant that the work of redemption was accomplished.

7. "Father, into thy hands I commend My spirit" (Lk 23:46).

THE BURIAL OF JESUS (Mt 27:57-61; Mk 15:42-47; Lk 23:50-56; Jn 19:38-42). Christ's burial took place immediadely after His death. Although the Romans allowed the bodies of those crucified to remain on the cross until devoured by beasts or birds of prey or until they became corrupt, the Jews insisted upon burial before sunset (Dt 21:23).

After receiving the necessary permission, Joseph of Arimathea buried Christ in his own rock-hewn tomb nearby. A large rock was set before the entrance and soldiers were sent to guard the tomb lest the disciples should steal the body.

CHRIST'S RESURRECTION FROM THE DEAD (Mt 28:1-20; Mk 16:1-18; Lk 24:1-49; Jn 20:1-31; Act 1:4-8; 1 Cor 15: 5-7). Christ arose from the dead on the third day after His death, and on that day appeared to Mary Magdalene, the holy women, Peter, the two disciples on the way to Emmaus, and the assembled Apostles, St. Thomas being absent. The soldiers who guarded the tomb at the time of Christ's Resurrection were bribed by the Jewish priests to say that the disciples came by night and stole Christ's body while they were sleeping.

CHRIST'S ASCENSION INTO HEAVEN (Mk 16:19-20; Lk 24:50-53; Act 1:9-12). After remaining on earth forty days Christ took leave of His disciples who were assembled at the Mount of Olives near Bethany, ascended into heaven.

Consult Appendix VII — CHRONOLOGICAL TABLE OF THE SAVIOR'S LIFE.

CHAPTER XV

THE MIRACLES AND PARABLES OF CHRIST

Christ's Miracles

THE NATURE OF MIRACLES. Miracles are occurrences outside the course of nature, perceptible to the senses and effected directly by God alone. Saint Thomas Aquinas, in his Summa Theologica (I, q. 110, a. 4), tells us that "A miracle is that which is done by God outside the order of all created nature." Again, we might define miracles as sensible works, beyond the powers of nature and attributed to God alone as the principal cause. Although God is the principal cause, He may use any creature as an agent or instrumental cause.

It is not the purpose of this book to prove the possibility of miracles. It is sufficient to say that miracles are possible if they have occurred; but they have occurred, as anyone of unprejudiced mind may discover for himself by a sincere and thorough investigation. In our own times the cases of Lourdes and other famous shrines prove this point most conclusively.

To those who object that miracles are impossible because they change physical laws, we answer that since God has the power to make these physical laws, He certainly has the power to suspend them.

WHY MIRACLES. "Miracles are not an end in themselves but are intended to show either the truth of what is taught or the presence of God in the person who teaches. The object of Christ's miracles was to prove His Divinity so that men might come to salvation. Some of these miracles proved His Divinity in that the cures He wrought were such as could only have been done by Divine power..."[26]

THE MIRACLES OF CHRIST. Christ's miracles as recorded in the Gospels may be placed in the following categories: A-Miracles in the Domain of Nature; B-Miracles of Healing; C-The Raising of the Dead; D-The Expulsion of Demons. After mention of each miracle, we will give the location of its occurrence and the Gospel passages that recount it.

A—*Miracles in the Domain of Nature.*

1) The water is changed into wine.
   Cana of Galilee   Jn 2:1-11
2) The first miraculous draught of fishes takes place.
   Sea of Galilee   Lk 5:1-11
3) Christ calms the sea.
   Sea of Galilee   Mt 8:23-27; Mk 4:36-40; Lk 8:23-25
4) The first multiplication of the loaves of bread occurs.
   Bethsaida-Julius   Mt 14:13-21; Mk 6:34-44; Lk 9:
                         12-17; Jn 6:1-13
5) Jesus and Peter walk on the lake. Jesus calms the storm.
   Sea of Galilee   Mt 14:22-33; Mk 6:45-52; Jn 6:16-21
6) The second multiplication of the loaves takes place.
   East of the Sea of Galilee   Mt 15:32-39; Mk 8:1-10

7) A fish with a stater (a coin) in its mouth is taken from the water.
Sea of Galilee   Mt 17:23-26

8) Christ curses the barren fig tree which withers.
Mount of Olives   Mt 21:18-22; Mk 11:12-14; 20-26

9) The second miraculous draught of fishes takes place.
Sea of Galilee   Jn 21:1-14

B—*Miracles of Healing.*

1) The royal official's son is cured.
Capharnaum   Jn 4:46-54

2) Peter's mother-in-law is cured.
Capharnaum   Mt 8:14-15; Mk 1:29-31; Lk 4:38-39

3) The leper is cured.
Galilee   Mt 8:2-4; Mk 1:40-45; Lk 5:12-14

4) The cure of the paralytic let down through the roof takes place.
Capharnaum   Mt 9:1-8; Mk 2:1-12; Lk 5:18-26

5) The man with a withered hand is cured.
Capharnaum   Mt 12:9-14; Mk 3:1-6; Lk 6:6-11

6) The centurion's servant is cured.
Capharnaum   Mt 8:5-13; Lk 7:1-10

7) The woman with a hemorrhage is cured.
Genesareth   Mt 9:20-22; Mk 5:25-34; Lk 8:43-48

8) The cure of the two blind men takes place.
Capharnaum   Mt 9:27-30

9) The man is cured at the pool of Bethsaida.
Jerusalem   Jn 5:5-16

10) The deaf-mute is cured.
Coast of Tyre and Sidon   Mk 7:31-35

11) The blind man is cured.
Bethsaida   Mk 8:22-26
12) The man born blind is cured.
Jerusalem   Jn 9:1-34
13) The cure of the stooped woman takes place.
Judea   Lk 13:10-17
14) A man with dropsy is cured.
Perea   Lk 14:1-6
15) The ten lepers are healed.
Perea   Lk 17:12-19
16) Two blind beggars are cured.
Near Jericho   Mt 20:29-34; Mk 10:46-52; Lk 18:35-43
17) Malchus' ear is healed.
Garden of Gethsemani   Lk 22:50-51; Jn 18:10-11

C—*Raising from the Dead.*

1) The widow's son is raised from the dead.
Naim   Lk 7:11-17
2) Jairus' daughter is raised from the dead.
Capharnaum   Mt 9:18,23-25; Mk 5:22-24,35-43;
                         Lk 8:41-42;49-56
3) Lazarus is raised from the dead.
Bethany   Jn 11:1-44

D—*Expulsion of Demons.*

1) A demoniac is cured in the synagogue.
Capharnaum   Mk 1:23-27; Lk 4:33-36
2) Two demoniacs are cured.
Geras   Mt 8:28-34; Mk 5:1-15; Lk 8:27-35

3) The possessed daughter of a Syro-Phoenician woman is cured.

Coast of Tyre and Sidon   Mt 15:21-28; Mk 7:24-30

4) A lunatic boy is cured.

Mt. Thabor (Mt. Hermon?)   Mt 17:14-20; Mk 9: 14-28; Lk 9:37-43

5) A blind and dumb demoniac is cured.

Capharnaum   Mt 12:22

✿   ✿   ✿

We might mention here some of the miracles connected with Christ Himself:

1) Christ escapes the mob which tried to hurl Him over the precipice.

Nazareth   Lk 4:28-30

2) The Transfiguration of Christ takes place before Peter, James, and John.

Mt. Thabor (Mt. Hermon?)   Mt 17:1-8; Mk 9:2-8; Lk 9:28-36

3) Jesus escapes His enemies who attempt to stone Him.

Temple in Jerusalem   Jn 8:59

4) The soldiers fall back to the ground when Jesus tells them that He is Jesus of Nazareth.

Garden of Gethsemani   Jn 18:4-6

5) Christ rises from the dead.

Jerusalem   Mt 28:6; Mk 16:6; Lk 24:6; Jn 20:5-9

6) Christ ascends into Heaven.

Mount of Olives   Mk 16:19; Lk 24:50-51

Other references to Christ's miracles will be found in: Mt 8:16-17, 15:30-31, 21:14; Mk 1:32-34; Lk 4:40, 6:18-19.

The Parables of Christ

MEANING OF A PARABLE. A parable is a story or account of some real or fictitious occurrence in human life or from nature that is used to illustrate a spiritual truth. At the time of Christ, and even before, it was customary for Jewish teachers to use parables or short comparisons for the sake of illustrating doctrine. The common people found that it was easier to comprehend a point presented to them in the form of a parable. Many abstract ideas were made clearer by means of the parable. St. Jerome tells us that the parable was a favorite form for the conveying of moral truths in Eastern countries.

A parable differs from a *fable* in this way: whereas the parable is always concerned with spiritual and supernatural truths, is heavenly in purpose, is always serious and reverent, and never speaks of or refers to nature in a figurative sense, a *fable* never rises higher than human morality and natural wisdom, refers to earthly things, often indulges in jests and mockings and often distorts nature, as in presenting talking beasts.

A parable differs from a *myth* as follows: whereas in a parable the illustration and the truth illustrated are always kept distinct, in a *myth* there is no distinction made between the truth and its vehicle. It also distorts the facts of nature and does not teach spiritual lessons.

A *proverb* is sometimes called a condensed parable and the Gospels do not distinguish between them, the Evangelists often using the terms interchangeably.

A *parable* differs from an *allegory* in this manner: whereas a parable needs an interpreter from without and its meaning is not certain before it is finished, an allegory is an extended metaphor which interprets itself as it proceeds. Christ's account of the Good Shepherd (Jn 10:11ff) would be an example of this.

WHY DID CHRIST USE PARABLES? Christ was using the ordinary method of instruction of the day when He taught in parables.

He realized that from the sensible and material things of the world, human knowledge proceeds to the insensible and immaterial, to the spiritual.

In the beginning of His Public Life Christ did not teach by parables. His teaching on the Kingdom of God was simple and plain, made known by His words and miracles. When unbelievers and persons ill-disposed to Him began openly to take a stand against Christ, then He began to use parables. These were advantageous to His followers insofar as they illustrated for them in a clear natured manner the truths He wished to reveal; they enabled the faithful to recall them more easily later, and they encouraged inquiry about what was not fully understood.

As for those people who did not deserve to know them and had become incapable of receiving them, the parables would veil the mysteries of the Kingdom of God. The Jewish leaders and majority were deserving of this punishment because they were hostile to Christ and His teachings. In concealing His doctrines by means of parables, Christ also acted mercifully since He spared the unbelievers the responsibility of knowing the truth and then rejecting it or profaning it. He also afforded them the opportunity of recalling what He had said by means of parables, if they later became well-disposed.

"THE KINGDOM OF HEAVEN." Since Christ began many of His parables with the phrase "Kingdom of Heaven" or "Kingdom of God," we might well consider what these phrases really mean. According to the rabbinical views of the time, the phrases, "Kingdom of Heaven," "Kingdom of God," "Kingdom of Yahweh" really meant the same thing.

"Kingdom of Heaven" was more popular among the Jews on account of the traditional reverence which precluded mention of the name of God. Possibly this is why St. Matthew, writing his Gospel for the Jews of Palestine, retains the phrase "Kingdom of Heaven," while St. Mark and St. Luke, who wrote their Gospels for pagan converts, use the phrase "Kingdom of God."

In the O. T., the "Kingdom of God" represented God's universal rule over all creatures, the Hebrew nation ("a priestly nation" Ex 19:6), and the universal, perpetual, indestructible, Messianic Kingdom which would be instituted by the Messias and which would bring peace and holiness.

In the N. T., the Kingdom of God or the Messianic Kingdom is established by Jesus Christ. It is primarily spiritual, admittance to it being achieved through repentance, Baptism, faith in Christ's message, and obedience to the Commandments. This Kingdom pertains to the present and the future insofar as it extends from the order of grace to the order of glory. Its establishment on earth is but preparatory to its final consummation in heaven.

This Kingdom will be universal, embracing all people. It is the Church of Christ established upon the rock foundation of Peter, the first Pope. This Kingdom is a true and real one, which embraces the Church Triumphant (those in heaven), the Church Suffering (the souls in Purgatory) and the Church Militant (those on earth fighting to overcome temptation and sin).

"THE KINGDOM OF GOD" IN PARABLES. The parables of the Kingdom stress the central idea of the Kingdom of God under various aspects. It indicates a new period of world history; it is being established by Christ; the Kingdom imposes duties and obligations on its members; it will develop in the course of time; it will find its consummation in heaven. (Cf. Steinmueller and Sullivan, *Catholic Biblical Encyclopedia*).

NUMBER AND CLASSIFICATION OF THE PARABLES. To determine the exact number of parables is difficult. If we include proverbial sayings and allegories there are more than seventy parables.

Authors differ as to the classification of the parables. We will follow the arrangement given by Charles J. Callan, O.P., in his book "The Parables of Christ."[27]

Part I. Eight Parables on the Kingdom of God.

    1) The Sower
            Mt 13:3-9,18-23; Mk 4:3-9,13-20; Lk8:5-8,11-15
    2) The Seed Growing Secretly
                                    Mk 4:26-29
    3, 4) The Mustard-Seed and The Leaven
            Mt 13:31-33; Mk 4:30-32; Lk 13:18-21
    5) The Hidden Treasure
                                      Mt 13:44

6) The Pearl of Great Price

Mt 13:45,46

7) The Good Seed and the Darnel Weed or Cockle

Mt 13:24-30,36-43

8) The Fishing-Net

Mt 13:47-50

Part II. Fifteen Parables on the Members of the Kingdom of God

9) The Great Harvest and the Few Laborers

Mt 9:37,38; Lk 10:2

10) The Bridegroom and the Wedding Guests

Mt 9:14,15; Mk 2:18-20; Lk 5:33-35

11) The Wayward Children

Mt 11:16-19; Lk 7:31-35

12, 13) Uprooted Plants and Blind Leaders

Mt 15:13,14; Lk 6:39

14) The Children and the Dogs

Mt 15:26,27; Mk 7:27,28

15-17) The Kingdoms of Christ and Satan

Mt 12:25-29,43-45; Mk 3:23-27; Lk 11:17-26

18) The Two Sons

Mt 21:28-32

19) The Wicked Tenants

Mt 21:33-46; Mk 12:1-12; Lk 20:9-19

20) The Royal Wedding-Banquet

Mt 22:2-14

21) The Grand Banquet

Lk 14:16-24

22) The Laborers in the Vineyard

Mt 20:1-16

23) The Closed Door

Lk 13:23-30

Part III. Twenty-Five Parables on Duties in the Kingdom of God

24) The Tree and Its Fruit

Mt 7:16-20; Mt 12:33-35; Lk 6:43-45

25) The Barren Fig-Tree

Lk 13:6-9

26) The Friend Coming at Midnight

Lk 11:5-8

27) The Son Who Asks His Father for Bread

Mt 7:9-11; Lk 11:11-13

28) The Unjust Judge

Lk 18:1-8

29) The Pharisee and the Publican

Lk 18:9-14

30) The Two Debtors

Lk 7:40-43

31) The Salt of the Earth

Mt 5:13; Mk 9:50; Lk 14:34,35

32, 33) The Lamp on the Lampstand and a City on a Hill

Mt 5:14-16; Mk 4:21; Lk 8:16; Lk 11:33

34) The Mote and the Beam

Mt 7:3-5; Lk 6:41,42

35) Pearls before Swine

Mt 7:6

36) The Good Samaritan

Lk 10:30-37

37) The Unmerciful Servant

Mt 18:23-35

Part IV. *Eight Parables on the Consummation of the Kingdom of God*

52) The Faithful Servant

Mt 24:45-51; Lk 12:42-48

53) The Ten Virgins

Mt 25:1-13

54) The Talents

Mt 25:14-30

55) The Gold-Pieces

Lk 19:12-27

56) Unprofitable Servants

Lk 17:7-10

CHAPTER XVI

THE PAULINE EPISTLES

New Testament Epistles in General

THE didactic or instructive books of the N. T. consist of twenty-one Epistles or letters. These letters were written to churches, e.g., St. Paul's Epistle to the Romans, or to individuals, e.g., St. Paul's Epistle to Timothy. The fourteen written by St. Paul are called by the name of the group or person to whom they were addressed. The remaining seven, called Catholic or General Epistles, because they were intended for the Church at large, are called by the name of the writer. The Catholic Epistles consist of the Epistle of St. James, the two of St. Peter, the three of St. John, and the one of St. Jude.

St. Paul's Epistles

Paul's Epistles as arranged in the N. T., seem to follow an order which was established at the beginning of the fourth century and was based on the importance and length of the letters, not on their chronology. There are two exceptions to this, however. The Epistle to the Ephesians follows the Epistle to the Galatians, although it is a little longer than the latter. Hebrews seems to have been placed last because before the fourth century there were some doubts as to its authenticity unofficially expressed.

"As to his style, St. Paul professes to hold in considerable contempt the art of the rhetoricians, and it is quite evident that he did not consciously strive after literary perfection. Yet there are passages in his Epistles where he reaches the heights of sublimity and eloquence, such as the thirteenth chapter of 1 Corinthians, the concluding verses of the eighth and the eleventh chapters of Romans. All students of Paul agree that his little letter to Philemon is a literary gem. In other passages he is lyrical, as in the latter part of 1 Corinthians 15.

"But on the other hand, the Apostle is often careless of the rules of good writing. He dictated his Epistles to a scribe or secretary, and often his thoughts run faster than his words. Thus he sometimes neglects to complete a sentence; at other times he introduces one relative clause after another which complicate and obscure the thought, or he throws in long parentheses. This carelessness of style is one of the causes of the difficulty of understanding the Apostle's writings.

"Another cause is that his letters teem with allusions to circumstances, persons, and situations of which we know nothing, save what we can gather from the vague references to them in the Epistles themselves. The letters of Paul, someone has said, are like a telephone conversation: we hear only one of the two persons engaged in the exchange of words.

"A third cause of the difficulty in understanding the

Apostle is that he at times gives a brief statement of doctrine which he had already set forth at length to his converts in sermons, instructions, and conversations. There is no intention on the part of the Apostle to present a systematic or a complete statement of Christian doctrine. His letters are occasional, i.e., they were called forth by some problem of discipline or doctrine, and their object is to explain further and clarify what had already been expounded fully by word of mouth.

"Yet, in spite of the difficulty of understanding St. Paul, there are many passages which easily yield a satisfactory and a sublime meaning. His Epistles are a mine of information on the beliefs and practices of the early Church. They give us precious data on Grace, the Sacraments, the Redemption, the Incarnation, the future life, and all the basic dogmas of the Christian faith."[28]

A Brief Biography of St. Paul

Paul, often called "Apostle of the Gentiles" because he worked primarily with non-Jewish peoples, was born in the early years of the Christian era. His family came from Tarsus, the capital of Cilicia. He himself says that he was the son of a Pharisee (Act 23:6) and from the tribe of Benjamin (Rom 11:1). At the time of his circumcision he was given the name Saul in memory of the first king of Israel who belonged to the same tribe. He inherited Roman citizenship through his father. In his Epistles he always used the Roman name, Paul.

Paul, who was a tent-maker by trade (Act 18:2-3),

was trained in the religious ideas of the Pharisees. Though
he may not have been allowed to attend the pagan schools
of Tarsus, he did acquire a knowledge of Greek and also
of profane authors. He left Tarsus for Jerusalem where he
studied the Scriptures and the Law under the famous Rabbi
Gamaliel I. He probably returned to Tarsus before the
call of St. John the Baptist and the beginning of Christ's
public ministry, since he makes no mention in his Epistles
of personally being acquainted with the Baptist or Christ
during His mortal life.

Not long after Christ's Crucifixion, Paul returned to
Jerusalem where he found a flourishing Christian community. His love and zeal for the Law made him a persecutor of the Christians. He witnessed and approved the
stoning of the first martyr, St. Stephen. He received authorization from the High-priest to seek out the Christians of
Damascus in Syria and bring them to Jerusalem.

As Paul came closer to Damascus, a great light sud-
denly enveloped him; blinded, he was thrown from his
horse. The glorified Christ appeared, saying: "Saul, Saul,
why dost thou persecute Me?" And he said: "Who are
thou, Lord?" And He said: "I am Jesus, whom thou are
persecuting. It is hard for thee to kick against the goad."
(Act 9:4-6) Christ instructed Paul to go to Damascus where
the once zealous persecutor of the Christians became a
Christian through baptism administered by Ananias.
Through the imposition of Ananias' hands, Paul's sight was
restored.

Shortly after his baptism, Paul withdrew into Arabia,
where he lived alone for perhaps two years, praying and
meditating on the Christian mysteries. He then returned to
Damascus where he incurred the enmity of the Jews be-

cause he preached the Divinity of Christ. Escaping from the enraged Jews, Paul visited St. Peter in Jerusalem, staying there fifteen days. When the Jews became aroused again, he was sent to Tarsus where he made many converts.

Paul made three principal missionary journeys, during which he established churches in the Near East and Europe. During these journeys he was accompanied at different times by Barnabas, John Mark, Silas, Timothy, and Luke. Paul's missionary journeys were most fruitful; he converted countless numbers and established churches to which he later wrote. His work and teachings were confirmed by miracles. While carrying out his mission, he endured great hardships and suffered persecution at the hands of the Jews and others stirred up against him.

At the Apostolic Council held in Jerusalem, Paul contended that Gentiles were exempt from the necessity of circumcision and other observances of Old Testament legal prescriptions. Peter and James agreed with him.

While preaching in the Temple at Jerusalem, Paul was recognized by some Jews, who, charging him with having brought Gentiles into the sacred area, beat him and dragged him out of the temple. He was arrested by Roman soldiers and kept in prison by Felix, the procurator of Caesarea. Porcius Festus, the successor of Felix, would have sent him back to the Jews had not Paul, exercising his right as a Roman citizen, appealed for a trial before Caesar. Paul was brought to Rome and finally acquitted after two years of imprisonment.

After his release, Paul probably went to Spain and other districts. We know nothing of the circumstances which led to his final arrest and removal to Rome. Paul was condemned to death, and being a Roman citizen, was beheaded, according to early tradition, on June 29, A.D. 67, at a place now called Tre Fontane.

According to 1 Cor 9:1, Paul was divinely chosen to be an Apostle. His feast is celebrated on June 29, together with that of St. Peter.

Cf. Appendix VIII — CHRONOLOGY OF ST. PAUL'S LIFE.

The Epistle to the Romans

Because of the doctrinal importance of its contents and because of the important position the Roman congregation held in the Church, St. Paul's Epistle to the Romans heads the New Testament Epistles. It was written at Corinth during the winter of A.D. 57-58 at the close of St. Paul's third missionary journey.

This is the only Epistle written by Paul which is addressed to a church not founded by him or one of his immediate co-workers. In the Epistle which served as his first contact with the Roman Christians, Paul informs them of his plans to visit them on his way to Spain (Rom 15:24).

PURPOSE OF THE EPISTLE. The purpose of the Epistle is to remind the Roman community that "I am not ashamed of the gospel, for it is the power of God unto salvation to everyone who believes, to Jew first and then to Greek. For in it the justice of God is revealed, from faith unto faith, as it is written. He who is just lives by faith." (Rom 1:16-17).

BRIEF CONTENT ANALYSIS: *Dogmatic Part* (1:16-11:36). The grace of justification is offered to all believers and to them alone. Theme of the dogmatic part, i.e., justification through faith (1:16-17). 1. The necessity of justification through faith (1:18-4:25). 2. The excellence of justification through faith is shown by the effects or fruits it produces (5:1-8:39). 3. The relation of the Gospel to the promises made to Israel. Answer to objections (9:1-11:36).

Hortatory Part (12:1-15:13). Various precepts and admonitions. 1. General admonitions, intended for all (12:1-13:14). 2. Conduct of Christians towards the weak in faith (14:1-15:13).

The First Epistle to the Corinthians

Corinth, a Roman colony in Greece, was, at the time of the Apostle, a prosperous but morally corrupt city. Paul founded the church there in the course of his second missionary journey. He remained at Corinth for about two years and when he left, the Church was developing rapidly. He was in communication with the Corinthians.

In 1 Cor 5:9-12, Paul alludes to a letter which was written to the Corinthians prior to the two we now possess. The First Epistle to the Corinthians would really be the "Second."

The Epistle was written from Ephesus, during Paul's third missionary journey, probably in the spring of A.D. 57.

PURPOSE OF THE EPISTLE. When Paul was at Ephesus, certain domestics from Corinth acquainted him with conditions of the Church there. Factions had formed about various preachers of the Gospel; incestuous Christians were giving scandal; lawsuits between Christians were being brought before pagan courts. To settle these problems and to answer certain questions concerning marriage and virginity, idol offerings, the manner of conducting religious gatherings, charisms (spiritual gifts), and their use, and the resurrection of the dead, Paul wrote his Epistle to the Corinthians.

BRIEF CONTENT ANALYSIS: *First Part* (1:10-6:20). Abuses are corrected. 1. Dissensions at Corinth (1:10-4:21). 2. Association with sinners (5:1-13). 3. Litigations before pagan judges (6:1-11). 4. Fornication and licentiousness (6:12-20).

Second Part (7:1-15:59). The Apostle replies to questions on six topics proposed by the Corinthians. 1. Matrimony and celibacy (7:1-40). 2. Partaking of idolothytes i.e., things sacrificed to idols (8:1-11:1). 3. Headdress of women in religious assemblages (11:2-16). 4. Decorum in celebrating the agape (11:17-34). 5. The various charisms or gifts of the Holy Spirit (12:1-14:40). 6. The future resurrection of the just (15:1-58).

The Second Epistle to the Corinthians

Paul wrote this letter to the Church of Corinth from Macedonia, a country north of Greece. He was most likely at Philippi at the time. This Epistle was written in the late fall of A.D. 57, towards the close of his third missionary journey.

The Epistle is one of the most intensely personal of Paul's writings. Vehement and intensely polemical, especially in the last four chapters, the writer would have his critics and adversaries know that he is a true Apostle of Jesus Christ, and that his sincerity and authority have been attested by heaven and by his labors and sufferings for the sake of the Gospel.

PURPOSE OF THE EPISTLE. Paul's primary purpose in writing this Epistle was to reestablish harmony between himself and the Corinthians and to refute the charges of inconstancy and insincerity on his part because of a visit which he had announced but had not made. He also wished to exhort the Corinthians to contribute to the relief of the poor Christians of Jerusalem. Finally he hoped that what he had written would bear fruit and that he would have to commend only good when he arrived at Corinth.

BRIEF CONTENT ANALYSIS: *In the Apologetic Part* (1:15-7:16). St. Paul defends his conduct against the calumnies of adversaries. 1. The charge of levity and inconstancy (1:15-2:17). 2. The charge of arrogance and pride (3:1-4:6). 3. The Apostles' motives in the performance of the duties of their ministry (4:7-6:10). 4. Conclusion to the apologetic part (6:11-7:16).

In the Hortatory Part (8:1-9:15) St. Paul speaks of the collection for the poor of the Church at Jerusalem. 1. St. Paul announces the collection (8:1-15). 2. St. Paul's agents in this matter (8:16-9:5). 3. Exhortation to cheerful generosity (9:6-15).

In the Polemical Part (10:1-13:10) St. Paul refutes the

pseudo-apostles and vindicates his apostolic authority. 1. St. Paul asserts his apostolic authority (10:1-18). 2. The Apostle affirms his superiority to his adversaries (11:1-12:10). 3. Conclusion of the polemical part (12:11-31:10).

The Epistle to the Galatians

The Galatians were sprung from Gallic or Celtic tribes which came east from the west and north of Europe in the third century B.C. Crossing the Alps they reached Rome in 390 B.C., crossed the Danube and invaded Macedonia and Greece in 278 B.C., and finally settled in the mountainous districts of Asia Minor. These districts took the name of the inhabitants—Galatia. In 25 B.C., Galatia became a Roman Province.

"Three answers have been proposed to the questions as to when, where, and to whom was this Epistle written. The MIXED THEORY assumes that Paul addressed the Christians of the whole Roman Province of Galatia from Corinth on his second missionary journey (50-52-53). This is scarcely probable because the Epistle implies that its readers are located in a circumscribed area, and are not scattered over Asia Minor. The NORTHERN GALATIAN THEORY assumes that the Epistle is addressed to the true Galatians, the inhabitants of primitive Galatia, while the Apostle was at Ephesus on the third missionary journey (53-54-58). There is a long tradition in favor of this theory... Those who hold the South Galatian Theory assert that the Epistle was written at Antioch prior to the Apostolic Council."[29]

PURPOSE OF THE EPISTLE. The purpose of the Epistle
is to refute the error of the Judaizers who troubled the faith
of the Galatians by preaching to them the necessity of ob-
serving the Mosaic Law, especially as to circumcision. Paul
also wished to show that the Law was a provisory institution and that through Christ's coming its role was ended.

BRIEF CONTENT ANALYSIS: *In the Apologetical Part* (1:
11-2:21) St. Paul proves the divine and apostolic origin
of his doctrine. 1. The divine origin of his doctrine (1:11-
24). 2. His doctrine is the same as that of the other Apostles
(2:1-21).

In the Dogmatic Part (3:1-4:21) St. Paul shows that
the Law does not confer the promises made to Abraham.
Three arguments prove this thesis. 1. The uselessness of
the Law and the importance of faith as a means of justification is evident to the Galatians from their own experience
(3:1-7). 2. The uselessness of the Law is proved by the
nature of the promises made to Abraham (3:8-4:20). 3. The
uselessness of the Law is proved by a typical explanation
of the history of the sons of Abraham (4:21-31).

In the Hortatory Part (5:1-6:10) St. Paul deduces practical conclusions and admonitions from the foregoing. 1.
Practical conclusions (5:1-25). 2. Special admonitions (5:
26-6:10).

The Epistle to the Ephesians

Scholars differ as to the identity of the recipients of
this Epistle. Some hold that the Epistle was sent as a cir-

cular letter to a group of churches of the Province of Asia, of which Ephesus was the capital. Others hold that the Epistle was written to the Church of Laodicea, but because of their wickedness, the name was deleted during the second century and the name of a more respected church, such as that of Ephesus, substituted.

This Epistle was written probably A.D. 63, towards the close of Paul's first Roman imprisonment. Because of this it is usually classified with the group of Captivity Epistles.

OCCASION AND PURPOSE OF THE EPISTLE. "Since personal allusions are absent, it is impossible to formulate any but the most general statement of the occasion upon which this Epistle was written. Perhaps Epaphras who had been in charge of the Church at Colossae also brought a report about some of the other Asiatic communities (cf. Eph 1:15; Col 1:7f), and thereupon Paul decided to send these communities an Epistle stressing the unity of the universal Church and urging them to strive for a still closer incorporation in Christ (Eph 2:19)."[30]

BRIEF CONTENT ANALYSIS: *The Dogmatic Part* (1:3-3:21)is developed in the form of thanksgiving and prayer. 1. The Apostle gives thanks in general for all favors conferred upon himself and the Ephesians (1:3-14). 2. In particular he thanks God for the Ephesians' perseverance in the faith (1:15-2:22). 3. The Apostle prays that they may persevere in their vocation (3:1-21).

Hortatory Part (4:1-6:9). 1. Practical conclusions from the foregoing (4:1-16). 2. Exhortation for all (4:17-5:20). 3. Exhortations for the Christian family (5:21-6:20).

CHAPTER XVII

THE PAULINE EPISTLES (Continued)

The Epistle to the Philippians

IN St. Paul's day Philippi was the capital of a district of Macedonia. Because of its site on the Egnatian Way linking Rome and the East, it was also a trade center. It was a military colony whose citizens enjoyed the special privilege of *jus italicum,* the full rights of those living in Italy itself.

Philippi was the first European city to be evangelized by Paul. The Philippian converts were so dear to him, that the Church at Philippi can be called his favorite.

Paul wrote this Epistle during his Roman imprisonment (A.D. 63).

PURPOSE OF THE EPISTLE. When Epaphroditus, after having recovered from his grave illness, was preparing to return to Philippi, Paul took the occasion to send to the Philippians, news and counsels.

BRIEF CONTENT ANALYSIS: *In the Historical Part* (1:12-2:30) St. Paul gives them information regarding himself, adding admonitions. 1. Information regarding himself (1:

12-26). 2. Admonitions (1: 27-2:18). 3.Concerning Timothy and Epaphroditus (2:19-30).

In the Hortatory Part (3:1-4:7) they are warned against the dangers threatening them from the Judaizers. 1. Dangers threatening the Philippians (3:1-4:1). 2. Special admonitions (4:2-7).

The Epistle to the Colossians

St. Paul did not, in person, found the Church of Colossae in the Roman Province of Asia just as he did not found himself the neighboring churches of Laodicea and Hierapolis. Paul's collaborator, Epaphras (Col 1:7;4:12-13) preached the Gospel in these regions. Probably it was information brought by Epaphras which led Paul to write this letter.

The Epistle was written during the Roman captivity of St. Paul in the spring of A.D. 63.

PURPOSE OF THE EPISTLE. Paul wrote this Epistle to warn the Colossians against the tendency towards superstition and rabbinical traditions and to counteract the work of false teachers who belittled the character and office of Christ and gave undue prominence to angels, holding that we must have access to God through them.

BRIEF ANALYTICAL CONTENT: *Dogmatic-Polemical Part* (1:13-2:23). 1. The Apostle shows the dignity of Christ, the Redeemer (1:13-23). 2. They must beware of heretics (1:24-2:23).

Hortatory Part (3:1-4:6). 1. General exhortation (3:1-17). 2. Special exhortation (3:18-4:6. Cf. Eph 5:22-6:9).

The First and Second Epistles to the Thessalonians

Paul founded the Church of Thessalonica (modern Salonica) in Macedonia during his second missionary journey when, from Troas in Asia Minor, he had gone into Europe for the first time. Thessalonica, an important harbor on the Thermaic Gulf, possessed a Jewish synagogue in which Paul preached for three successive Sabbaths, converting some Jews and a good number of "God-fearing" Gentiles, among whom was an important group of noble women. The Church of Thessalonica was composed mostly of converts of pagan origin.

The success of Paul's apostolate (and also that of Silas and Timothy who worked with him) aroused the unbelieving Jews who hired disreputable characters to stir up the people against Paul and his assistants. To save the missionaries from mob violence, the Christians prevailed upon them to go to Borea. From Borea, Paul went to Athens and after making two unsuccessful attempts to return to Thessalonica, he sent Timothy in his place while he himself went to Corinth.

While at Corinth Paul wrote both Epistles probably A.D. 51-52. These Epistles are generally believed to be the first canonical Epistles written by St. Paul.

PURPOSE OF THE EPISTLES. The First Epistle was written to praise the faith and perseverance of the Thessalonian Christians and to condemn their immorality, their idleness, their pagan vices, and their confused ideas about the Parousia, i.e., the Second Coming of Christ.

The Second Epistle was written to dispel the doubts and allay the fears of the Thessalonians who were confirmed in their belief that the Parousia was imminent.

CONTENT ANALYSIS OF FIRST THESSALONIANS: *In the Historical Part* (2:1-3:13) St. Paul depicts the friendly relations that have existed between Thessalonians and himself. 1. Their mutual relations during his sojourn with them (2:1-16). 2. Manifestations of his love and affection for them during his absence (2:17-3:13).

In the Hortatory Part (4:1-5:22) St. Paul exhorts them to avoid sin and practice virtue; instruction on the parousia. 1. Exhortation to avoid sin (4:1-12). 2. Instructions on the second coming of Christ (4:13-15:11). 3. Additional exhortations (5:12-22).

CONTENT ANALYSIS OF SECOND THESSALONIANS: *In the Dogmatic Part* (2:1-17) St. Paul treats of the second coming of Christ. *Hortatory Part* (3:1-15).

The Pastoral Epistles

The title "Pastoral Epistles" is given to three Epistles written by Paul to his disciples and co-workers, Timothy and Titus, the former receiving two and the latter one. They differ from Paul's other Epistles in that they are not addressed to any particular church but rather to individuals. They are called "Pastoral" because they were written to pastors of churches and treated, among other things, of the duties of their office.

Timothy was at Ephesus when Paul wrote the First Epistle to him probably from Macedonia in A.D. 65 or 66 and the Second Epistle probably from Rome in A.D. 66 or 67.

Titus was in Crete when Paul wrote to him about A.D. 65 or 66. The place of composition is uncertain, but scholars suggest Nicopolis in Epirus, Corinth, or Macedonia.

CONTENT ANALYSIS OF FIRST TIMOTHY: 1. St. Paul gives his disciple several rules on preaching (1:3-20). 2. Precepts regarding public prayer (2:1-15). 3. Qualities required in the ministers of the Church (3:1-13). 4. Instructions for Timothy (3:14-4:16). 5. Duties of a bishop towards the members of the Church (5:1-6:2). 6. Special admonitions for Timothy (6:3-21).

CONTENT ANALYSIS OF SECOND TIMOTHYS 1. The Apostle exhorts Timothy to fidelity and fortitude (1:6-2:13). 2. Repetition of precepts to be observed in the performance of pastoral duties (2:14-4:18).

CONTENT ANALYSIS OF THE EPISTLE TO TITUS: 1. The qualities requisite in a candidate for the priesthood (1:5-16). 2. St. Paul exhorts Titus to remind the Christians of their duties (2:1-15). 3. General exhortations (3:1-11).

The Epistle of Philemon

Paul sent this personal letter to his friend Philemon, a prominent Christian of Colossae, whom Paul had converted.

When Onesimus, one of Philemon's slaves, ran away and went to Rome, he met Paul and was converted to Christianity. Paul sent the slave back to Philemon with the Epistle which was also addressed to Apphia, Philemon's wife. In the letter Paul tactfully requests Philemon to deal kindly with his run-away slave, now a fellow Christian, and he hints at the emancipation of the slave. The Epistle was probably written in A.D. 63.

The Epistle to the Hebrews

"The question of the Pauline authorship of the Epistle is obscure and controvertible. Both internal and external evidence can be adduced to support or challenge its authenticity.

"The most probable solution of this problem has been given by Origen. He distinguishes between the author and the actual writer or redactor. According to his suggestion, Paul, the inspired author, is responsible for the ideas and content; the inspired secretary was responsible for the literary form. The actual writer may have been Clement of Rome, Luke, Barnabas, Apollos, Aristion, Aquila, or Priscilla. This opinion is in accord with three decisions made by the Pontifical Biblical Commission on June 24, 1914."[31]

The use of Greek words, expressions, etc., point to the fact that this Epistle was written in Greek. Many scholars consider the Epistle's style to be the best in the N. T. O. T. quotations are taken from the Septuagint.

It seems probable that this Epistle was addressed to

Jewish Christians, since its theme and mode of argumentations support a knowledge of the O. T. in its readers and familiarity with Jewish religious institutions and customs.

The identity of the recipients of this Epistle is uncertain. The Churches of Rome, Alexandria, or Jerusalem have been proposed.

The place of composition was probably Italy, and more precisely Rome. It was written before the destruction of Jerusalem A.D. 70 and after the death of James the Less in A.D. 62.

PURPOSE OF THE EPISTLE. The purpose of the author in writing this Epistle was to exhort and comfort the faithful who had undergone persecution and who were still under its threat, in order to avert the danger of defection and apostasy, and to encourage faith, hope, and perseverance.

BRIEF CONTENT ANALYSIS: *In the Dogmatic Part* (1:1-10:18) the greater excellence of the New Testament as compared with the Old Testament is demonstrated. 1. The authors of the two Testaments (1:1-2:18). 2. The mediators of the two Testaments (3:1-4:13). 3. The high priest of the N. T., is compared with the high priests of the O. T. (4:14-10:18).

In the Hortatory Part (10:19-13:21) St. Paul exhorts his readers to perseverance in the faith and to the practice of various virtues. 1. Perseverance in faith (10:19-12:13). 2. Various virtues which should adorn them as Christians (12:14-13-21).

CHAPTER XVIII

THE CATHOLIC EPISTLES. THE APOCALYPSE

THE CATHOLIC EPISTLES are the seven non-Pauline Epistles. The Muratorian Fragment (2nd century) applies the term "Catholic Epistles" to Jude and the two Epistles of John. Dionysius of Alexandria (190-265) included under this term the First Epistle of John. Origen (c. 185-254) applied the term to First Peter, First John, and Jude, Eusebius (265-340) applied it to the whole group and by St. Jerome's time (c. 331-420) it was customary to speak of "the seven Catholic Epistles."

These Epistles are called "Catholic" because they were not addressed to an individual Church, but were intended for the Church at large. Although the Second and Third Epistles of John were addressed to individuals, they have been classified with the First, probably because of their common authorship.

The Epistle of St. James

It is commonly held that the author of this Epistle is the Apostle James, the son of Alpheus of Cleophas (Mt 10:

3) and Mary, sister or close relative of the Blessed Virgin. For this reason, he was sometimes called "the brother of the Lord." St. James the Less or Younger, as he is called to distinguish him from the other Apostle, James the Greater, held a distinguished position in the early Christian community at Jerusalem. According to tradition he was the first Bishop of Jerusalem. Tradition tells us that he was martyred in A.D. 62 when the Jews threw him from a wing of the temple. His feast is celebrated May 11, together with St. Philip.

James wrote his Epistle to Christians (probably of Jewish origin) outside of Jerusalem, hoping to guide and direct them against the temptations and difficulties they were encountering in the midst of paganism.

It probably was written from Jerusalem sometime between 58 and 62.

In the fifth chapter James speaks of the Sacrament of Extreme Unction.

BRIEF CONTENT ANALYSIS: *In the First Part* (1:19-2:26) the Apostle teaches that not faith only, but also good works are necessary. *In the Second Part* (3:1-4:12) St. James warns the Christians against imprudent zeal in teaching others. *In the Third Part* (4:13-5:18) St. James gives special admonitions.

The First and Second Epistles of Peter

Peter, the author of these two Epistles, who originally was called Simon, was the son of Jona. He was a fisherman from Bethsaida, a town on Lake Tiberias. He later settled at Capharnaum. Peter was introduced to Christ by his brother Andrew. Both gave up all to follow Christ. Christ appointed Peter head of His Church. Peter was honored on many occasions by Christ. He continued to rule the Church, dwelling in Rome for many years as its first Bishop. He was crucified with his head downwards in A.D. 67 at Rome. His feast is celebrated on June 29.

Peter wrote the First Epistle to Gentile Christians of the northern part of Asia Minor. He wrote it from "Babylon," a cryptic designation for Rome, in the latter part of A.D. 63 or the beginning of A.D. 64. Peter's purpose in writing this Epistle was to encourage the Christians in the true faith and against the abuse and oppression of their pagan neighbors.

The Second Epistle was written to the same people from Rome during 66 or 67, shortly before his death. The contents of this Epistle, especially Chapter 2, resemble those of the Epistle of St. Jude so strikingly that it seems probable Peter was familiar with Jude's Epistle and made use of some of its thoughts. Peter's purpose in writing this Epistle was to caution the faithful against false teachers and to encourage them to persevere in their faith.

CONTENT ANALYSIS OF FIRST PETER: *In the First Part* (1:13-2:10) St. Peter exhorts his readers, in a general way, to lead a good Christian life. *In the Second Part* (2:11-4:19) St. Peter gives general and special admonitions to all the Christians. *In the Third Part* (5:1-11) more particular admonitions are given.

CONTENT ANALYSIS OF SECOND PETER: *In the First Part*

(1:3-21) St. Peter treats of the magnitude of the gifts conferred by Christ, and the solidity of the foundation on which the Christian faith rests. *In the Second Part* (2:1-3:13) the Christians are admonished to avoid the company of heretics.

The Three Epistles of St. John

St. John the Apostle, the author of the Fourth Gospel, is the author of three short Epistles, the first one consisting of five chapters, the second and third consisting of thirteen and fifteen verses respectively.

John was the son of Zebedee, a fisherman of Bethsaida, and Salome, one of the Galilean women who served Christ and His Disciples. John and the Apostle, James the Greater, were brothers. John was the favorite Apostle of Christ, receiving many privileges. After the Descent of the Holy Ghost, Peter and John labored in Jerusalem and Samaria. Towards the end of his life John was exiled to the island of Patmos. According to tradition, he alone of the Apostles died a natural death during the reign of Trajan (98-117).

His feast is observed on December 27 and that of St. John before the Latin Gate on May 6.

John wrote his First Epistle probably to the Christians of Asia Minor towards the end of the first century during his last years at Ephesus. His purpose was to combat the false teachings of those who distinguished between Jesus and Christ, of those who reduced Christ's humanity to a mere appearance, and of those who did not think that Christ was the real Messias.

The Second Epistle was probably composed at the same time and from the same place as the First Epistle. This Epistle was written not to an individual but probably to a local congregation situated in Asia Minor. John stresses his favorite theme of fraternal love and warns against certain false teachers.

John wrote his Third Epistle probably from Ephesus towards the end of the first century to a Gaius about whom nothing is known. In the letter John praises Gaius for his virtues and censures Diotrephes for showing himself rebellious against John's authority.

CONTENT ANALYSIS OF FIRST JOHN: *In the First Part* (1:5-2:29) St. John refers to the Gospel (Jn 1:4-10), announcing that God is life. *In the Second Part* (3:1-4:6) St. John refers to a second teaching of the Gospel (Jn 1:12), viz., Christ gave "power to be made the sons of God to them that believe in His name" (3:1-2). Three conditions requisite in the sons of God. *In the Third Part* (4:7-5:12) they are reminded of a third Gospel truth: "Love moved God to give His only begotten Son" (Jn 3:-16).

The Epistle of St. Jude

Jude, the author of this Epistle, was an Apostle, a relative of Christ and the brother of James the Less. He is also known as Thaddeus. According to tradition Jude labored in Arabia, Syria, and Mesopotamia and suffered martyrdom at Beirut. His feast is kept on October 28.

The Epistle was probably written from Palestine between 62 and 67. It was probably written to Jewish Christians. The author warned them against false teachers.

BRIEF CONTENT ANALYSIS: *In the First Part* (5-16), describing the false teachers and referring to the fate that awaits them, St. Jude cautions his readers against their doctrines. *In the Second Part* (17-23) he admonishes the faithful to be mindful of the teachings of the Apostles.

The Apocalypse of St. John the Apostle

This is the only prophetic book in the N. T. Its title is Greek and means a "revelation." The Apocalypse is a revelation of things that were and will be.

St. John the Apostle and Evangelist wrote this book while he was in exile on the island of Patmos in the Mediterranean Sea. He wrote it probably in A.D. 96. It consists of a circular letter to seven churches of the Roman Province of Asia: Ephesus, Smyrna, Pergamus, Thyatira, Sardis, Philadelphia, and Laodicea. Through these churches it would reach all the Christian communities in Asia, ultimately becoming the property of the universal Church.

"It must be remembered that the Apocalypse is written in symbolic language, and that each series of seven symbols repeats or recapitulates its predecessors, giving a general picture of the whole history of the Church on earth. Although many of the symbols were taken from contemporary history and from the Roman Empire, yet these contemporary events are but symbols of all similar events down through the centuries."[32]

PURPOSE OF THE WORK. John wrote to stimulate the faith and fortitude of the Christians of these seven churches. They are told that persecution has come and greater persecutions will follow, but the victory of the Church is certain. John warns the people against the dangers of being seduced and of becoming morally lax.

BRIEF CONTENT ANALYSIS: *First Septenary* (1:9-3:22). Seven letters to the churches of Asia. 1. A preparatory vision (1:9-20). 2. The seven letters: to Ephesus (2:1-7), Smyrna (2:8-11), Pergamus (2:12-17), Thyatira (2:18-29), Sardis (3:1-6), Philadelphia (3:7-13), Laodicea (3:14-22).

Second Septenary (4:1-8:1). The seven seals. 1. A preparatory vision (4:1-5:14). 2. Opening of the first six seals: the white horse, war (6:1-2), the red horse, strife (6:3-4), the black horse, famine (6:5-6), the pale horse, pestilence (6:7-8), the souls under the altar (6:9-11), the earthquake (6:12-17). 3. An intermediary vision (7:1-17). 4. Opening of the seventh seal: the silence (8:1).

Third Septenary (8:2-11:19). The seven trumpets. 1. The preparatory vision (8:2-6). 2. The first six trumpets: the earth set on fire (8:7), the sea turned into blood (8:8-9), the streams become bitter (8:10-11), the heavenly bodies darken (8:12-13), the woe of locusts (9:1-12), the woe of horsemen (9:13-21). 3. An intermediary vision (10:1-11:13). 4. Sounding of the seventh trumpet: the third woe (11:14-19).

Fourth Septenary (12:1-15:4). The seven signs. The vision of: 1. The woman and the dragon (12:1-18). 2. The beast rising out of the sea (13:1-10). 3. The beast rising

from the earth (13:11-18). 4. The Lamb and the virgins
(14:1-5). 5. The three angels (14:6-13). 6. The harvest
and the vintage (14:14-20). 7. The seven angels and the
song of triumph (15:1-4).

Fifth Septenary (15:5-16:21). The seven bowls. 1. A
preparatory vision (15:5-8). 2. The first six bowls are
poured out of the earth (16:1-2), the sea (16:3), the waters
(16:4-7), the sun (16:8-9), the throne of the beast (16:10-
11), the Euphrates (16:12). 3. An intermediary vision (16:
13-16). 4. Pouring out of the seventh bowl upon the air
(16:17-21).

Sixth Septenary (17:1-19:8). The destruction of Babylon. Seven stages of the prophecy: 1. Description of Babylon (17:1-6). 2. Explantion of Babylon (17:7-18). 3. Fall
of Babylon (18:1-8). 4. Mourning of Babylon (18:1-8).
5. Final ruin of Babylon (18:21-24). 6. Song of praise at
its fall (19:1-5).: 7. God's reign and the marriage of the
Lamb (19:6-8). Epilogue (19:9-10).

Seventh Septenary (19:11-22:5). The Consummation.
Seven visions: 1. The Conqueror and his hosts (19:11-16).
2. The defeat of the beast (19:17-21). 3. The victory of
Satan (20:1-10). 4. The general judgment (20:11-15).
5. The new Jerusalem 21:1-8). 6. The plan of the new
Jerusalem (21:9-27). 7. The paradise of God (22:1-5).

Epilogue (22:6-21). 1. The attestation of the angel
(22:6-9). 2. The time is near (22:10-15). 3. The final attestation; blessing (22:16-21).

APPENDICES

Appendix I

PLAINS, SEAS, MOUNTAINS, AND RIVERS
OF THE HOLY LAND

(Taken from "Maps of the Holy Land" by E. Seraphim, O.F.M. and J. Kelly, O.F.M., St. Anthony Guild Press, Paterson, N. J., 1947, pp. 54-56).

Plains of the Holy Land

The Plain of Accho (*Acre, Akka*): Extends from the northern base of Mount Carmel northward to the headland Ras en-Naqourah, called of old "Ladder of the Tyrians." The plain is 20 miles long and 4 miles wide. The ancient city of Accho, which in our Lord's day bore the Greek name of Ptolemais (cf. Acts 21:7), was about midway in its length.

The Plain of Esdraelon: The Graecized form of Jezrahel. This plain, shaped like an irregular triangle, is in the central range, and bounded on the north by the Galilean hills, on the east by the mountains of Gelboe (Gilboa), and on the south and west by the Samarian hills and Mount Carmel.

In the east, the plain divides into three arms: one to the northeast, passing between Mount Thabor and Mount Moreh; another going eastward to the Jordan Valley, between Mount

Moreh and Mount Gelboe; the third going southward toward Engannim.

The middle arm is the one famed in Israelitic history.

The Plain of Philistia: Extends 40 miles southward from the Plain of Saron, and is 10 to 15 miles wide.

The Plain of Saron: Extends from 4 miles north of Caesarea in Samaria, to 9 miles south of Jaffa. It is 46 miles long and 6 to 12 miles wide.

SEAS OF HOLY LAND

The Dead Sea: About 47 miles long; 6 to 10 miles wide; 1,300 feet below the Mediterranean level; 1,220 feet at its greatest depth. It contains no life whatsoever. Jebel Ousdoum is a mountain of salt on the southwest side of the Sea. Other names for the Dead Sea: "Sea of Salt" (Cf. Gn 14:3); "Sea of Arabah" or "of the Plain" (Deut. 3:17); "East Sea" or "Former Sea" (Ezech. 47:18); "Lake Asphaltites" (Greek name); Mare Mortuum (Latin name); Bahr Lout, "Sea of Lot" (modern Arabic name).

The Sea of Galilee: Fourteen miles long; 6 to 7 miles wide; 600 feet below the Mediterranean Sea; 160 feet at its greatest depth. It is fresh water. Other names for the Sea of Galilee: "Lake Kinneret" (Hebrew Kinnor, "Harp"); "Sea of Genesar" (after the Captivity); "Sea of Genesareth" (Matt. 14:34); "Sea of Tiberias" (John 6:1); Bahr Tabariyeh (modern Arabic name).

Lake Houleh: Four miles long; 4 miles wide; 7 feet above the Mediterranean level; 10 to 16 feet deep. Its water is fresh. Other names for Lake Houleh: "Waters of Merom" (Jos. 11:5); "Lake Semechonitis" (Josephus); Bahr el-Houleh (modern Arabic name).

MOUNTAINS OF THE HOLY LAND

(The height given in each case represents the distance above sea level).

Mount of Beatitudes: Tradition points out two places as the site of the Sermon on the Mount: (1) Qoroun Hattin (Horns of Hattin), 1,191 feet high; (2) a site two miles north of Ain Tabigah called Shejerat el-Moubarakat ("Blessed Trees" or "Trees of Blessing"), 825 feet high. Some archaeologists would place the site on the northeast section of the Sea of Galilee in Wady Joramayah.

Mount Calvary: Calvary is in the west section of the city of Jerusalem. The Hebrew term is Golgotha (Cf. John 19:17). In 135, the Emperor Hadrian built a pagan temple upon this site. In 325, St. Helena caused two churches to be erected on the site, one on Calvary and the other over the Holy Sepulchre. The present structure, incorporating both, was built by the Crusaders in 1140-1149. The rock of Calvary measures 14 feet high and 22 feet long; the summit is 2,550 feet above sea level.

Mount Carmel: Carmel means "Park" in Hebrew. Other names are the Arabic Jebel Qormul and Jebel Mar Elias ("Mount of St. Elias"). It is 1,782 feet high. Cf. III Kings 18:19.

Mount Garizim: The name signifies "People Living in the Desert" in Hebrew. Also called Jebel et-Tour ("Mount of Holiness") and Jebel as-Samire ("Mount of Samaria" in Arabic). It is 2,800 feet high. Cf. Deut. 11:29; Jos. 8:33 and John 4:20.

Mount Gelboe: Important in Old Testament history, this group of hills, about 1,700 feet high, forms part of the eastern boundary of the Plain of Esdraelon. Cf. I Kings 31:1-8.

Mount Hebal (Ebal): Ebal means "Bare" in Hebrew. This mount is also called Jebel Eslamiyeh in Arabic. It is 3,095 feet high. Cf. Deut. 11:29 and Jos. 8:33 (Mount of Curses).

Mount Hermon: Hermon means "Lofty" in Hebrew. Also called Jebel es-Sheikh ("Mount of the Sheik") and Jebel et-Tour ("Mount of Holiness") in Arabic. Some scholars regard this mountain as the scene of the Transfiguration. Cf. Matt. 17:1-7. It is 8,811 feet high.

Horns of Hattin: The name in Arabic is Qoroun Hattin. See Mount of Beatitudes.

Mount Lebanon: Lebanon means "White" in Hebrew. Together with Hermon, Lebanon forms a rampart to the north of Palestine. The highest point of the range is Jebel Makmal, 10,200 feet. Cf. II Par. 2:8-16.

Mount Moreh (Little Hermon): Also called Jebel el-Dahy in Arabic. It is 1,815 feet high. Cf. Luke 7:11.

Mount Moriah: The Hebrew meaning is "Given by God." The mount, in the eastern section of Jerusalem, was bought by King David (II Kings, chapter 24: I Par., chapter 21) for the site of the Temple (II Par., chapter 3). It is now the site of the Moslem Mosque of Omar. It is 2,450 feet high.

Mount Nebo: Means "Lofty Place" in Hebrew. Also called Jebel Neba in Arabic. It is 3,960 feet high. Cf. Deut., chapter 34, Ras Siagha (Phasga, Pisgah) is near this mountain.

Mount of Olives (Mount Olivet): The scene of Christ's weeping over Jerusalem (Luke 19:37-41); the Palm Sunday procession (Matt. 21:1-9); and the Ascension (Acts 1:9-12). Gethsemani and the Tomb of the Virgin are at the foot of the Mount of Olives. It is 2,650 feet high. Arabs call it Jebel el-Tour ("Mount of Holiness").

Jebel Ousdoum: This is a mountain of salt on the southwest shore of the Dead Sea. It is 7 miles long, 1½ to 2 miles wide. The top is covered with 20 feet of marl, with 70 to 160 feet of pure salt beneath. A vivid imagination can see a figure of Lot's wife on the side of the hill.

Mount Scopus: A northward continuation of the Mount of Olives, more than 2,700 feet high, Scopus was named from a Greek word meaning "Watchman" or "Sentinel." It is the site of the modern Hebrew University.

Mount Sinai: Although not in Palestine, this mountain is included here because of its unique part in Jewish history. In Hebrew its name signifies "Pointed." Arabs call it Jebel Musa ("Mount of Moses") and Tour Sina ("Point of Holiness"). It is 8,551 feet high. Cf. Exod. 19:20.

Mount Sion (Zion): Means "Arid" in Hebrew. Mount Sion, site of the original "City of David," at one time harbored the Ark of the Covenant. The word "Sion" was often used in poetic allusion to signify the city of Jerusalem or the whole Jewish people. The exact location of Sion has led to controversy. The southwestern section of Jerusalem, accepted for centuries, has been abandoned by some modern archaeologists in favor of the hill of Ophel, south of the Temple area.

Mount of Temptation: Also called Jebel Quarantal ("Mount of the Forty") in Arabic. It is 990 feet high. Cf. Luke 4:1-15.

Mount Thabor: Means "Height" in Hebrew. Also called Jebel et-Tour ("Mount of Holiness") in Arabic. The traditional site of the Transfiguration. It is 1,850 feet high. Cf. Judg. 4:14; Mark 9:1-8.

RIVERS OF THE HOLY LAND

Jordan: The Hebrew term Yarden and the Arabic El-Our-doun mean "Descender." Another Arabic name for this river, Esh-Sheriat el-Kebir, signifies "The Great Watering-place." The sources of the Jordan are:

1. Mount Hermon at the Hesbani Springs.
2. Dan (Tell el-Quadi).
3. Caesarea Philippi (Banias).

Salient featuers of the Jordan: From the Hesbani Springs to Lake Houleh (the Waters of Merom), 40 miles; from Lake Houleh to the Sea of Galilee, 15 miles; from the Sea of Galilee to the Dead Sea, 79 miles. Total 134 miles in a direct line, and about 200 in a winding course.

Drop per mile, 22 feet.
Width, 80 to 180 feet.
Depth, 8 to 12 feet.

Arnon: The Hebrew meaning is "Swift." The Arabic name is Wady Modjib. Cf. Num. 21: 13.

Jabbok: A Hebrew word which signifies "Pouring Out." Cf. Num. 21:24. The Arabic name is Nahr ez-Zerka.

Cedron: The meaning is unknown; a probable conjecture is "Black." Cf. II Kings 15:23.

Cison: The Hebrew meaning is "Tortuous." The Arabic name is Nahr el-Mouqatta. Cf. Judg. 4:7.

Sorek: This signfiies in Hebrew the "Choice Vine." The Arabic name is Wady Sourar. Cf. Judg. 16:4.

Wady El-Qelt: An Arabic word meaning "Trench." Possibly the torrent of Carith. Cf. III Kings 17:3.

Wady Farah: Arabic name which signifies "Valley of Joy" or "Mouse." Scene of the Twenty-second Psalm.

Yarmuk: The Hebrew meaning is unknown. The Arabic name is Sheriat el-Menadireh, "The Drinking Trough of Mena-direh."

Zerka Main: The Hebrew name is unknown. The Arabic term signifies "Pouring Waters."

Appendix II

MIRACLES IN THE OLD TESTAMENT

(Taken from "Aids to the Study of the Bible" by Hugh Pope, O.P.,
P. J. Kenedy and Sons, N.Y.C., 1; pp. 126-127).

1-Ex 4:2-4. Moses' rod is turned into a serpent.

2-Ex 4:6-7. Moses' hand becomes leprous.

3-Ex 7-12. The ten plagues of Egypt.

4-Ex 13:21-22. The pillar of cloud and fire.

5-Ex 14. The passage of the Red Sea.

6-Ex 14:23-26. The healing of the waters of Mara.

7-Ex 16:13. The quails.

8-Ex 16:13-36. The Manna.

9-Ex 17:6. Water from the rock at Raphidim.

10-Ex 40:32-36. The "Glory" of the Lord, commonly termed by the Rabbis the "Shechinah."

11-Lv 9:24. Fire descends on the holocaust.

12-Lv 10:2. Fire destroys Aaron's sons, Nadab and Abiu.

13-Nm 11:1. Fire destroys the murmurers.

14-Nm 12:10. Mary is smitten with leprosy.

15-Nm 16:31. The earth opens and swallows Dathan and Abiron.

16-Nm 16:35. Fire destroys the children of Core.

17-Nm 17:1-10. Aaron's rod blossoms miraculously.

18-Nm 21:6-9. The fiery (venomous) serpent and the brazen serpent.

19-Nm 22:28-30. Balaam's ass speaks to him.

20-Jos 3:15-17. The miraculous passage of the Jordan.

21-Jos 6:20. The walls of Jericho fall.

22-Jos 10:12-14. The sun and the moon stand still.

23-1Sm 5:3-5. The pagan idol, Dagon, falls to the ground.

24-1Sm 5:6-15. Plagues on the Philistines.

25-1 Sm 6:19. The slaughter of those who looked into the Ark.

26-1 Sm 12:18. Thunder and rain out of due season at Samuel's prayer.

27-2 Sm 24. The plague, owing to the census of the people; its cessation.

28-3 Kgs 8:10. The "Shechinah" (cf. 10) on occasion of the consecration of Solomon's temple.

29-3 Kgs 13:4-6. The withering of Jeroboam's hand; its restoration at the prophet's prayer; the splitting of the altar.

30-3 Kgs 17. Elias calls a famine on earth; he is fed by ravens; he multiplies the oil and meal; he raises to life the widow's son.

31-3 Kgs 18:38,45. Elias calls down fire from heaven on the sacrifice, and wins rain by his prayers.

32-4 Kgs 1:10-12. Elias calls down fire from heaven on the two captains and their two bands of fifty.

33-4 Kgs 2. Elias strikes the waters with his mantle, thus making a passage way; Elias is taken up into heaven in a fiery chariot; his mantle descends on Eliseus, who crosses the Jordan by its means; Eliseus sweetens a spring of water; bears come and destroy his mockers.

34-4 Kgs 3:15-20. Eliseus supplies the troops with water in the desert.

35-4 Kgs 4. Eliseus multiplies the oil; he raises a child to life; he purifies the poisoned food; he multiplies food.

36-4 Kgs 5. Naaman is miraculously healed in the Jordan; his leprosy attaches itself to Giezi, Eliseus' servant, because of his dishonesty.

37-4 Kgs 6:5-6, 18-20. Eliseus makes the iron head of an axe float; he blinds the Syrian troops and leads them into Samaria.

38-4 Kgs 13:21. The bones of Eliseus miraculously give life to a dead man.

39-4 Kgs 19:35. An angel slays 85,000 of Sennacherib's troops.

40-4 Kgs 20:1-11. Ezechias' life is prolonged by fifteen years, the shadow on the dial of Achaz going back ten degrees in proof of this.

41-2 Par 7:1 Fire descends on Solomon's holocausts.

42-2 Par 14:12. Asa gains a miraculous victory over the Ethiopians.

43-2 Par 26:19. Azarias is miraculously inflicted with leprosy.

44-Dn 1:15. The health of Daniel and his companions is miraculously preserved.

45-Dn 3:24,48,91-93. The miraculous preservation in the furnace of Sidrach, Misach, and Abdenago.

46-Dn 5:5. The writing on the wall of the palace of Baltassar.

47-Dn 6:22. Daniel in the lions' den.

48-Dn 13:45-50. Daniel's miraculous knowledge.

49-Dn 14. Daniel again in the lions' den.

50-2 Mc 3:24-26;33-34. The divine punishment of Heliodorus; he is miraculously healed.

Appendix III

A CHRONOLOGY OF HEBREW HISTORY

(There are no positive dates for many of the events of Jewish history, particularly early history. Even our most recent Catholic Scripture works are not always in agreement. The dates given below and generally taken from the work of Fr. Daniel W. Martin, C.M.; "A Guide to Old Testament History" (Kenrick Seminary, St. Louis, Mo., 1951) would seem to represent a fair cross-section of the opinions offered.

Person or Event	B.C.
Abraham	c. 2000
Joseph in Egypt	c. 1700
Moses and the Exodus from Egypt	c. 1300-1290
Josue and the Conquest of Canaan	c. 1250
Period of the Judges	c. 1200-1020
Reign of Saul	c. 1020-1004
Reign of David	c. 1004-965
Reign of Solomon	c. 965-926
Division of the Kingdom: Israel and Judah	c. 926
Fall of Samaria (kingdom of Israel Destroyed)	721
Fall of Jerusalem (kingdom of Judah becomes a Province of Babylon)	587
Beginning of Exile	?
Restoration of the Jews	c. 539
Dedication of the Second Temple	516
Desecration of the Temple	175
Revolt of the Macabees	?
Jerusalem Falls to Pompey (Judea Made a Tributary to Rome)	63
Birth of Christ	7

Appendix IV

SOME MESSIANIC PROPHECIES

1. *Hope of a Redeemer*: "Arise, be enlightened, O Jerusalem; for thy light is come, and the glory of the Lord is risen upon thee. For behold darkness shall cover the earth, and a mist the people; but the Lord shall rise upon thee, and His glory shall be seen upon thee. And the Gentiles shall walk in thy light, and the kings in the brightness of thy rising." (Is 60: 1-3)

2. *The Virgin Birth*: "Behold a virgin shall conceive, and bear a son, and his name shall be called Emmanuel." (Is 7:14)

3. *Christ's Divine Attributes*: "A child is born to us, and a son is given to us, and the government is upon his shoulders; and his name shall be called Wonderful, Counsellor, God the Mighty, the Father of the World to come, the Prince of Peace." (Is 9:6)

4. *The Birthplace of Christ*: "And thou, Bethlehem Ephrata, art a little one among the thousands of Juda; out of thee shall He come forth unto me that is to be the ruler in Israel; and his going forth is from the beginning, from the days of eternity." (Mi 5:2)

5. *The Flight into Egypt*: "I called my Son out of Egypt." (Os 11:1)

6. *Shepherd of the Flock*: "I will set up one shepherd over them, and he shall feed them, ...and he shall be their shepherd." (Ez 34:23)

7. *Miraculous Cures*: "Then shall the eyes of the blind be opened, and the ears of the deaf shall be unstopped. Then shall the lame man leap as a hart, and the tongue of the dumb shall be free. For waters are broken out in the desert, and the streams in the wilderness." (Is 35:5-6)

8. *Messianic Preaching*: "The spirit of the Lord is upon me,

because the Lord hath anointed me: he hath sent me to preach to the meek, to heal the contrite of heart, and to preach a release to the captives, and deliverance to them that are shut up; to proclaim the acceptable year of the Lord, and the day of vengeance of our God; to comfort all that mourn; to appoint to the mourners of Sion, and to give them a crown for ashes, the oil of joy for mourning, a garment of praise for the spirit of grief..." (Is 61:1-3)

9. *Lowliness*: "Behold my servant, I will uphold him: my elect: my soul delighteth in him. I have given my spirit upon him, he shall bring forth judgment to the Gentiles. He shall not cry, nor have respect to person, neither shall his voice be heard abroad. The bruised reed he shall not break, and smoking flax he shall not quench; he shall bring forth judgment unto truth." (Is 42:1-3)

10. *Palm Sunday*: "Rejoice greatly, O daughter of Sion: shout for joy, O daughter of Jerusalem. Behold thy king will come to thee, the just and saviour; he is poor, and riding upon an ass, and upon a colt the foal of an ass." (Za 9:9)

11. *The Betrayal*: "They weighed for my wages thirty pieces of silver." (Za 11:12)

12. *The Sacrifice and Priesthood of the New Law*: "For from the rising of the sun even to the going down, my name is great among the Gentiles, and in every plice there is sacrifice, and there is offered to my name a clean oblation, for my name is great among the Gentiles, saith the Lord of Hosts." (Mal 1:11)

"The Lord hath sworn, and he will not repent: "Thou art a priest forever according to the order of Melchisedech." (Ps 109:4)

13. *Christ's Passion:* "They shall look upon me whom they have pierced." (Za 12:10) "What are these wounds in the midst of thy hands?" (13:6) "Strike the shepherd, and the sheep shall be scattered." (13:7)

14. *Christ's Resurrection*: "Because thou will not leave my soul in hell; nor wilt thou give thy holy one to see corruption." (Ps 15:10)

15. *Christ's Ascension:* "The Lord saith to my Lord: 'Sit thou at my right hand until I make thy enemies thy footstool'." (Ps 109:1)

BIBLICAL CALENDAR, MONEY, AND MEASURES

(Taken from the National Catholic Almanac, 1955. Published by St.
Anthony's Guild, Paterson, N. J., 253)

BIBLICAL CALENDAR

The basic unit of the Biblical Calendar was the day. Prior
to the Babylonian Exile, the Jews divided the day into the
three periods of morning, midday, and evening; after the Exile
they adopted the more prevalent division of the day into two
periods of twelve hours. The first hour was 6:00 A.M.; the third,
9:00 A.M.; the sixth, 12 o'clock noon, etc. The night was divided
into four watches: 6:00 to 9:00 P.M., 9:00 P.M. to 12 o'clock
midnight, 12 to 3:00 A.M., 3:00 to 6:00 A.M. The weeks consisted of seven days, which were numbered; only the seventh
day was named, the Sabbath. There were twelve months in
the year, called lunar months because their computation was
based on the cycles of the moon. The names of the months were:

Abib or Nisan (April)   Tishri or Ethanim (October)
Ijar (May)   Marhhescevan (November)
Sivan (June)   Chisleu (December)
Thammuz (July)   Tebeth (January)
Ab (August)   Sheba (February)
Elul (September)   Adar (March)

Veadar was an intercalary month, coming every three years.

BIBLICAL MONEY AND COINS

Before the Babylonian Exile there is no trace of money but only of weights. Gold and silver were weighed in the balance by means of little stones, models and examples of which were preserved in the Tabernacle (Exodus 30:13). After the exile there is frequent mention of Hebrew coins. Pagan coins, too, were used.

Mite	¼ cent	Tribute	31.5 cents
Farthing	½ cent	Stater or Sicle	51 cents
Farthing	1 cent	Light Shekel, silver	40 cents
Gerah or Obol	2¼ cent	Heavy Shekel, gold	80 cents
As	from 1 to 16 cents	Shekel, gold	$12.88
Penny	17 cents	Manah, silver	$20.24
Groat	17 cents	Manah, gold	$323.95
Drachma	17 cents	Talent, silver	$1,214
Piece of Silver	50 cents	Talent, gold	$19,440
Didrachma	30 cents		

BIBLICAL MEASURES OF LENGTH

The unit was a cubit (forearm) divided into:

Finger	.75 in.	Span	9.00 in.
Palm	3.00 in.	Building cubit	17.1 in.
A Sabbath Day's journey		2,000 cubits or 3,600 ft.	
Ezekiel's Reed		10 ft.	

BIBLICAL DRY MEASURE / BIBLICAL LIQUID MEASURE

Log	1.00 pints	Log	1.00 pints
Cab	4.00 pints	Cab	2 quarts
Omer	7.20 pints	Hin	1.50 gallons
Seah	1.50 pecks	Bath	9.00 gallons
Ephah	4.50 pecks	Kor	90.00 gallons
Kor	11.25 bushels	(Measures are approximate)	

HARMONY OF THE FOUR GOSPELS

(Taken from "The New Catholic Edition of the Holy Bible," published by the Catholic Book Publishing Co., New York, N. Y.)

PART I

The Hidden Life of Our Lord

Subject	Matthew	Mark	Luke	John
Prologue			1, 1-4	
The Word: Divine Nature and Mission of Jesus				1, 1-14
Annunciation of the Baptist			1, 5-25	
Annunciation of the Savior			1,26-38	
The Visitation			1,39-56	
The Birth of the Baptist			1,57-80	
The Virgin Birth	1,19-25			
The Birth of Jesus			2, 1-20	
The Circumcision			2,21	
The Magi	2, 1-12			
The Presentation in the Temple			2,22-39	
The Flight into Egypt	2,13-18			
Genealogy of Jesus	1, 1-17		3,23-38	
The Child Jesus in the Temple			2,42-50	
The Return to Nazareth	2,19-23		2,51	
His Life at Nazareth			2,50-52	
John the Baptist	3, 1-10	1, 1-6	3, 1-14	1,28
1st Testimony of John the Baptist	3,11-12	1, 7-8	3,15-17	1,15
The Baptism of Jesus	3,13-17	1, 9-11	3,21-23	
The Temptation	4, 1-10	1,12-13	4, 1-13	
2nd Testimony of John the Baptist				1,19-28
3rd Testimony of John the Baptist				1,29-34

PART II

The Beginning of His Public Ministry

Subject	Matthew	Mark	Luke	John
The First Disciples				1,35-51
The Marriage Feast at Cana (1st Miracle)				2, 1-11
Passage through Capharnaum				2,12
First Cleansing of the Temple				2,13-17
Jesus Answers the Jews				2,18-25
Nicodemus				3, 1-21
4th Testimony of John the Baptist				3,22-36
John the Baptist Is Imprisoned	14, 3-4	6,17-18	3,19-20	
Jesus Arrives in Samaria				4, 4-22
The Samaritan Woman				4
Jesus Withdraws to Galilee	4,12	1,14	4,14	4,43
Cure of the Official's Son				4,46-54
Jesus' Sojourn at Capharnaum	4,13-16			
Preaching Repentance	4,17		4,14-15	
First Miraculous Draught of Fishes and Definitive Vocation of the First Four Apostles	4,18-22	1,16-20	5, 1-11	
Jesus Preaches in the Synagogue at Capharnaum		1,21-22	4,31-32	
The Cure of a Demoniac		1,23-28	4,33-37	
Peter's Mother-in-law Cured	8,14-17	1,29-34	4,38-41	
Mission of Preaching and Miracles	4,23-26	1,35-39	4,42-44	
Sacrifice to Follow Christ	8,19-22		9,57-62	
The Storm on the Lake	8,23-26	4,35-40	8,22-26	
Expulsion of the Devils in Gerasa	8,28-34	5, 1-20	8,26-39	
Return to Capharnaum	9,1	2,1		
A Paralytic at Capharnaum	9, 2-8	2, 2-12	5,18-26	
The Call of Matthew	9, 9-13	2,13-17	5,27-32	
Jairus' Daughter and the Woman with a Hemorrhage	9,18-26	5,21-43	8,40-56	
Two Blind Men	9,27-31			
A Dumb Demoniac	9,32-34		11,14	
The Cure at the Pool of Bethsaida				5, 1-47

Subject	Matthew	Mark	Luke	John
The Plucking of Grain on the Sabbath	12, 1-8	2,23-28	6, 1-5	
A Man with a Withered Hand	12, 9-14	3, 1-6	6, 6-11	
The Mercy of Jesus	12,15-21	3, 7-12		
The Choice of the Twelve		3,13-19	6,12-16	
Sermon on the Mount: the Beatitudes	5, 1-12		6,17-49	
A Leper	8, 2-4	1,40-45	5,12-17	
The Centurion's Servant	8, 5-13		7, 1-10	
The Widow's Son at Naim			7,11-17	
The Baptist's Deputation	11, 1-30		7,18-35	
The Penitent Women			7,36-50	
The Ministering Women			8,2	
His Relatives Want to Lay Hold of Him		3,20-21		
The Dumb and Blind Demoniac	12,22-25	3,22-27	11,14-27	
Blasphemy against the Holy Spirit	12,31	3,28-30	12,10	
The Sign of Jonas	12,39-41			
The Ninevites and the Queen of Saba	12,42			
Jesus and His Brethren	12,46-50		8,20-22	
The Parable of the Sower	13, 3-23	4, 2-20	8, 4-18	
Purpose of This Teaching	5,15	4,21-25	8,16-18	
The Weeds	13,24-30			
The Seed Grows of Itself		4,26-29		
The Mustard Seed	13,31-32	4,30-34		
The Leaven	13,33			
The Hidden Treasure	13,44			
The Fine Pearls	13,45-46			
Parable of the Net	13,47-51			
Jesus Preaches at Nazareth	13,53-58	6, 1-6	4,16-30	
The Mission of the Apostles	9,35-38	6, 7-13	9, 1-6	
Death of the Baptist	14, 1-12	6,14-29	9, 7-9	
Jesus Feeds Five Thousand	14,13-21	6,34-44	9,12-17	6, 1-15
Jesus Walks on the Water	14,22-36	6,45-58		6,16-21
The Discourse on the Eucharist				6,22-72
Jesus and the Pharisees	15, 1-20	7, 1-23		
The Canaanite Woman	15,21-28	7,24-30		
Healing of a Deaf-Mute		7,32-37		
Jesus Feeds Four Thousand	15,32-39	8, 1-10		

Subject	Matthew	Mark	Luke	John
The Pharisees and Sadducees Ask a Sign	16, 1-4	8,11-13		
The Leaven of the Pharisees	16, 5-12	8,14-21		
Cure of a Blind Man at Bethsaida		8,22-26		
The Foundation of the Church	16,13-20	8,27-30	9,18-21	
Passion and Resurrection Foretold	16,21-28	8,31-39	9,22-27	
Jesus Transfigured	17, 1-13	9, 1-12	9,28-36	
A Possessed Boy	17,14-20	9,13-28	9,37-43	
The Second Prediction of the Passion	17,21-22	9,29-31	9,44-45	
Paying the Temple Tax	17,23-26			
Instruction on the Qualities of an Apostle	18, 1-5	9,32-40	9,46-50	
Avoiding Scandal	18, 6-11	9,41-50		
The Lost Sheep	18,12-14		15, 1-32	
Fraternal Correction	18,15-20			
The Unmerciful Servant	18,21-35			
Departure for Jerusalem			9,51	7, 2-13
Passing Through Samaria			9,52-56	
Ten Lepers			17,11-19	
Jesus Preaches in the Temple				7,14-53
The Adulteress				8, 1-11
Jesus Affirms His Divinity				8,12-59
The Man Born Blind				9,1-41
The Good Shepherd				10, 1-31
The Seventy-two Disciples			10, 1-20	
Return from the Mission			10,17-24	
Jesus Draws Men Gently to Himself	11,25-30		10,21-24	
Near Jericho: The Good Samaritan			10,25-37	
Bethany: Martha and Mary			10,38-42	
Mount of Olives: Lessons of Prayer			11, 1-13	
Denunciation of the Pharisees			11,37-54	
An Exhortation: The Rich Man with Abundant Crops			12, 1-59	
Penance: A Barren Fig Tree; A Parable			13, 1-21	
The Narrow Gate: Jesus and Herod			13,23-35	
In the House of the Pharisee on the Sabbath			14, 1-24	
At the Feast of the Dedication				10,22-42

Subject	Matthew	Mark	Luke	John
The Unjust Steward			16, 1-18	
The Rich Man and Lazarus			16,19-31	
Coming of the Kingdom of God			17,20-37	
The Godless Judge; The Pharisee and the Publican			18, 1-14	
The Question of Divorce	19, 1-12	10, 1-12	16,18	
Jesus Blesses the Children	19,13-15	10,13-16	18,15-17	
The Danger of Riches	19,16-26	10,17-27	18,18-27	
Reward Promised to the Apostles	19,27-30	10,28-31	18,28-30	
The Laborers in the Vineyard	20, 1-16			
The Raising of Lazarus				11, 1-44

PART III

The Last Days of Our Lord on Earth

Preludes

Subject	Matthew	Mark	Luke	John
The Council				11,45-46
Third Prediction of the Passion	20,17-19	10,32	18,31-34	
The Mother of James and John	20,20-28	10,35-45		
The Blind Men at Jericho	20,29-34	10,46-53	18,35-43	
Zaccheus the Publican			19, 1-10	
Parable of the Gold Pieces			19,11-27	
The Anointing at Bethany	26, 6-13	14, 3-9		12, 2-11
Sunday: Triumphal Entry into Jerusalem	21, 1-11	11, 1-11	19,29-44	12,12-19
Jesus Announces His Death				12,20-36
Jesus Returns to Bethany	21,17	11,11		
Monday: Jesus Curses a Fig Tree	21,18-19	11,12-14		
Cleansing of the Temple	21,12-16	11,15-18	19,45-48	
Jesus Returns to Bethany		11,19		
Tuesday: The Withered Fig Tree	21,20-22	11,20-26		
The Authority of Jesus	21,23-27	11-27-33	20, 1-8	
Parable of the Two Sons	21,28-32			
Parable of the Vine-dressers	21,33-46	12, 1-12	20, 9-19	
The Marriage Feast	22, 1-14			
Tribute to Caesar	22,15-22	12,13-17	20,20-26	
The Sadducees and the Resurrection	22,23-33	12,18-27	20,27-40	
The Great Commandment	22,34-40	12,28-34		
The Son of David and Lord of David	22,41-46	12,35-37	20,41-44	

204   GETTING TO KNOW THE BIBLE

Subject	Matthew	Mark	Luke	John
Hypocrisy of Scribes and Pharisees	23, 1-39	12,38-40	20,45-47	
The Widow's Mite		12,41-44	21, 1-4	
Prophecy Concerning Jerusalem and the End of the World	24, 1-51	13, 1-37	21, 5-28	
Parable of the Ten Virgins	25, 1-13			
Parable of the Talents	25,14-30			
The Last Judgment	25,31-46			
Reflections of St. John				12,37-50
Jesus Foretells His Coming Death	26, 1-12			
Wednesday: Conspiracy against Jesus	26, 3-5	14, 1-2	22, 1-2	
The Betrayal	26,14-16	14,10-11	22, 3-6	
Thursday: The Last Supper	26,20	14,17-25	22,14-18	
The Washing of the Feet				13, 1-20
The Holy Eucharist	26,26-28	14,22-24	22,19-20	
Who Is the Betrayer	26,21-25	14,18-21	22,21-23	13,21-23
The Betrayer				13,23-30
Contention among the Apostles			22,24-30	
The New Commandment				13,31-35
Peter's Denials Predicted	26,31-35	14,27-31	22,31-33	13,36-38
Discourse after the Last Supper				14-16
Christ's Priestly Prayer for Unity				17

The Passion

The Garden of Olives	26,36	14,32	22,39-40	18, 1
The Agony in the Garden	26,37-46	14,32-42	22,41-46	
Jesus Arrested	26,47-56	14,43	22,47-53	18, 2-12
Jesus before Annas				18,13-14
Jesus before Caiphas	26,57-58	14,53-54	22,54	18,15-16
Jesus Is Interrogated				18,19-23
False Witnesses	26,60-62	14,55-61		
Jesus the Son of God	26,63-68	14,61-65		
Peter's Denial	26,69-75	14,66-72	22,55-62	18,25-27
Jesus Is Mocked			22,63-65	
Friday: Jesus before the Sanhedrin	27, 1	15, 1	22,66-71	
Jesus Is Taken to Pilate	27, 2	15, 1	23, 1	18,28
The End of Judas	27, 3-10			
Jesus before Pilate	27,11-14	15, 2-5	23, 2-5	18,29-38
Jesus before Herod			23, 6-12	

Subject	Matthew	Mark	Luke	John
Barabbas Is Preferred to Jesus	27,15-26	15, 6-15	23,13-25	18,39-50
The Scourging and Crowning	27,26-31	15,15-20		19, 1-3
Behold the Man				19, 4-8
Pilate Interrogates Jesus Further				19,12
Jesus Is Condemned	27,26	15,15	23,23	19,13-16
Simon of Cyrene	27,32	15,21	23,25	
The Holy Women			23,27-31	
The Crucifixion	27,34-38	15,22-28	23,33	19,17-24
The Mother of Jesus				19,25-27
Jesus Is Derided	27,39-44	15,29-32	23,25-39	
The Good Thief			23,40-43	
The Last Words	27,50	15,37	23,46	19,28-30
The Death of Jesus	27,45-53	15,33-38	23,44-45	
The Centurion and Other Spectators	27,54-56	15,39-41	23,47-49	
Jesus Is Pierced with a Lance				19,31-37
The Burial	27,57-61	15,42-47	23,50-55	19,38-42
The Guarding of the Sepulchre	27,62-66			
Holy Women Prepare Spices and Ointments			23,56	
Saturday: The Women at the Grave		16, 1		

The Resurrection

Subject	Matthew	Mark	Luke	John
Sunday: The Resurrection	28, 1-2	16, 2-4	24, 1-2	20, 1
The Apparition of the Angel	28, 2-7	16, 5-7	24, 4-8	
Peter and John at the Sepulchre			24,12	20, 3-10
Jesus Appears to Magdalene		16, 9-10		20,11-18
Jesus Appears to the Holy Women	28, 8-10			
The Guards and the Chief Priests	28,11-15			
Emmaus		16,12-13	24,13-35	
Jesus Appears to Peter			24,34	
Jesus Appears to the Eleven			24,36-43	20,19-23
Jesus and Thomas				20,24-29
The Manifestation at the Sea of Tiberias				21, 1-24
Commission of the Apostles	28,16-20			
Apparition at Jerusalem; Last Words of Jesus		16,14-18	24,44-50	
The Ascension		16,19	24,51-53	
The Preaching of the Apostles		16,20		
Epilogue				21,24-25

APPENDIX VII

CHRONOLOGICAL TABLE OF THE SAVIOR'S LIFE

(Taken from the "National Catholic Almanac"—1952, 255)

The dates here given are approximate, for exact dates cannot be given for many events. Christ's birth is assigned to the year 7 B.C. Our Lord certainly was born before 4 B.C., when Herod died, because the king did not die until at least six months after the visit of the Magi, and Christ, scholars hold, was at least eighteen months old at Herod's death.

Date	Event
8 B.C.	Annunciation of the birth of John the Baptist (Lk 1:5-25)
7 B.C.	Annunciation of the birth of Christ (Lk 1:26-38).
	Visitation of Mary to her cousin Elizabeth (Lk 1:39-56).
	Birth of John the Baptist (Lk 1:57-66).
7 B.C.	Birth of Christ (Lk 2:1-7).
	Circumcision of Our Lord (Lk 2:21).
6 B.C.	Presentation of Christ in the Temple (Lk 2:22-38).
5 B.C.	Adoration of the Magi (Mt 2:1-12).
	Flight of the Holy Family into Egypt (Mt 2:13-15).
	Massacre of the Holy Innocents (Mt 2:16).
4 B.C.	Return of the Holy Family from Egypt (Mt 2:19-21).
4 B.C. to 27 A.D.	Hidden life of Christ (Mt 2:21-23; Lk 2:39-52).
7 A.D.	The Boy Jesus in the Temple (Lk 2:41-50).
27 A.D.	Beginning of John the Baptist's preaching (Mt 3:1-12; Mk 1:4-8; Lk 3:1-18).

Date		Event

28 A. D. Jan. — Baptism of Christ and beginning of His 40-day fast (Mt 3:13-17,4:2; Mk 1:9-13; Lk 3:21-22,4:1-2).

Mar. — First public miracle, performed at the marriage feast at Cana (Jn 2:1-11).

Celebration of first Passover and expulsion of the money-changers from the Temple (Jn 2:13-17).

Apr. — Early Judean ministry (Jn 3:22).

May — Beginning of Galilean ministry (Mt 4:12-25; Mk 1:14-45; Lk 4:14-45; Jn 4:43-54).

June — Choice of the Twelve Apostles (Mt 10:1-4; Mk 3:13-19; Lk 6:12-16).

Sermon on the Mount (Mt 5:1—7:29; Lk 6:20-49).

29 A. D. Mar. — Martyrdom of John the Baptist (Mt 14:1-12; Mk 6:14-29; Lk 3:19-20).

Apr. — The second Passover (Jn 6:4).

Aug. — The Transfiguration (Mt 17:1-9; Mk 9:1-8; Lk 9:28-36).

30 A. D. Apr. — Anointing at Bethany (Mt 26:6-13; Mk 14:3-9; Jn 12:1-8).

Final ministry in Jerusalem (Mt 21—25; Mk 11—13; Lk 19:29—21; Jn 12:12-50).

Apr. 2 Triumphal entry into Jerusalem (Mt 21:1-11; Mk 11:1-11; Lk 19:29-44; Jn 12: 12-19).

Apr. 5 Judas' agreement with chief priests to betray Jesus (Mt 26:14-16; Mk 14:10-11; Lk 22:3-6).

Apr. 6 The Last Supper and institution of the Holy Eucharist (Mt 26:20-29; Mk 14:17-25; Lk 22:14-20; Jn 13—17; 1 Cor. 11:23-25).

Agony in the Garden (Mt 26:36-46; Mk 14:32-42; Lk 22:39-46).

Apr. 7 Passion and Death (Mt 26:47—27; Mk 14:43—15; Lk 22:47—23; Jn 18—20).

Apr. 9 Resurrection (Mt 28:1-10; Mk 16:1-11; Lk 24:1-43; Jn 20:1-23).

May 18 Ascension (Mk 16:19-20; Lk 24:50-53; Acts 1:9-12).

May 28 Descent of the Holy Ghost (Acts 2:1-4).

CHRONOLOGY OF ST. PAUL'S LIFE

(Taken from "Paul the Apostle" by Giuseppe Ricciotti 124)

Dates (A.D.)	Events in Paul's Life	Documents	Paul's Writings
1-5	Birth of Paul	Acts 7:58; Philemon 9	
13-18 (?)	Beginning of studies in Jerusalem	Acts 22:3; 26:4	
36	Stoning of Stephen, Conversion of Paul	Acts 7:58; 9:1-19; 22:4-20; Gal 1:13-16	
36-39	Sojourn in Damascus, in Arabia, and again in Damascus	Acts 9:20-22; Gal 1:17; Acts 9:23-25	
39	First journey to Jerusalem, and fifteen day sojourn there	Acts 9:26-28; Gal 1:18-20	
39-43	Sojourn in Tarsus	Acts 9:29-30; Gal 1:21-24	
43-44	Sojourn in Antioch	Acts 11:25-26	
44	Famine, and journey (to bring the contributions) to Jerusalem	Acts 11:27-30; 12:25	
45-49 (50)	**First Missionary Journey - Cyprus and Asia Minor)**	Acts 13-14; 2 Tim 3:11	
49 (50)	Apostolic Council in Jerusalem	Acts 15:1-35; Gal 2:1-10	

49 (50)	Dispute with Cephas in Antioch	Gal 2:11ff	
(49) 50 (52) 53	**Second Missionary Journey** - (Asia Minor, Macedonia, Achaea)	Acts 15:36-18:22 (cf. Gal 4:13-15	
50 (51)	Philippi	Acts 16:11ff	
51	Thessalonica	Acts 17:1ff	1 Thessalonians
51-53	Corinth	Acts 18:1ff	2 Thessalonians
53-58	**Third Missionary Journey**	Acts 18:23-21:17	
53	Galatia-Phrygia	Acts 19:1ff	(54) Galatians (?)
54-57	Ephesus		(56) 1 Corinthians
57	Departure from Ephesus	Acts 20:1-6	2 Corinthians
	Sojourn in Macedonia		
	Journey to Illyria (Rom. 15:19)?		
57-58	Corinth (three winter months)	Acts 20:3	Galatians (?) Romans
58	Journey. Arrest in Jerusalem	Acts 20:3;23:25	
58-60	**Imprisonment in Caesarea**	Acts 24-26	
60-61	Sea voyage, shipwreck at Malta. Arrival in Rome	Acts 27-28:16	
61-63	**First Imprisonment In Rome**	Acts 28:17-31	Colossians, Ephesians, Philemon, Philippians
63-64	Journey in Spain		
64	Sojourn in Italy		Hebrews (?)
64-66	Journey in the Orient (Ephesus, Crete, etc.) Macedonia, Nicopolis	1 Tim 1:3; Titus 1:5;3:12	1 Timothy Titus
66-67	**Second Imprisonment in Rome**	2 Tim 1:15-18;4:9-21	2 Timothy
67	Martyrdom		

Appendix IX

EPISTLES AND GOSPELS FOR SUNDAYS AND HOLYDAYS, AND SAME NOTABLE FEASTS

SUNDAYS, ETC.	EPISTLES	GOSPELS
Advent, 1	Rom 13:11-14	Lk 21:25-33
Advent, 2	Rom 15:4-13	Mt 11:2-10
Advent, 3	Phil 4:4-7	Jn 1:19-28
Advent, 4	1 Cor 4:1-5	Lk 3:1-6
Christmas, Mass 1	Ti 2:11-15	Lk 2:1-14
Christmas, Mass 2	Ti 3:4-7	Lk 2:15-20
Christmas, Mass 3	Heb 1:1-12	Jn 1:1-14
St. Stephen	Act 6:8-10;7:54-59	Mt 23:34-39
St. John	Sir 15:1-6	Jn 21:19-24
Holy Innocents	Ap 14:1-5	Lk 2:13-18
St. Thomas	Heb 5:1-6	Jn 10:11-16
St. Sylvester	2 Tm 4:1-8	Lk 12:35-40
Circumcision	Ti 2:11-15	Lk 2:21
Holy Name of Jesus	Acts 4:8-12	Lk 2:21
Epiphany	Is 60: 1-6	Mt 2:1-12
Holy Family	Col 3:12-17	Lk 2:42-52
After Epiphany, 2	Rom 12:6-16	Jn 2:1-11
After Epiphany, 3	Rom 12:16-21	Mt 8:1-13
After Epiphany, 4	Rom 13:8-10	Mt 8:23-27
After Epiphany, 5	Col 3:12-17	Mt 13:24-30
After Epiphany, 6	1 Thes 1:2-10	Mt 13:31-35
Septuagesima	1 Cor 9:24-27;10:1-5	Mt 20:1-16
Sexagesima	2 Cor 11:19-33;12:1-9	Lk 8:4-15
Quinquagesima	1 Cor 13:1-13	Lk 18:31-43
Ash Wednesday	Jl 2:12-19	Mt 6:16-21
Lent, 1	2 Cor 6:1-10	Mt 4:1-11
Lent, 2	1 Thes 4:1-7	Mt 17:1-9
Lent, 3	Eph 5:1-9	Lk 11:14-28
Lent, 4	Gal 4:22-31	Jn 6:1-15
Passion Sunday	Heb 19:11-15	Jn 8:46-59

Palm Sunday	Phil 2:5-11	Mt 26:36-75;27:1-60
Maunday Thursday	1 Cor 11:20-32	Jn 13:1-15
Good Friday	Ex 12:1-11	Jn 18:1-40;19:1-42
Holy Saturday	Col 3:1-4	Mt 28:1-7
Easter Sunday	1 Cor 5:7-8	Mk 16:1-7
Easter Monday	Act 10:37-43	Lk 24:13-35
Easter Tuesday	Act 13:26-33	Lk 24:36-47
Low Sunday	1 Jn 5:4-10	Jn 20:19-31
After Easter, 2	1 Pt 2:21-25	Jn 10:11-16
After Easter, 3	1 Pt 2:11-19	Jn 16:16-22
After Easter, 4	Jas 1:17-21	Jn 16:5-14
After Easter, 5	Jas 1:22-27	Jn 16:23-30
Ascension Day	Act 1:1-11	Mk 16:14-20
Within the Octave	1 Pt 4:7-11	Jn 15:26;16:4
Whit-Sunday	Act 2:1-11	Jn 14:23-31
Whit-Monday	Act 10:42-48	Jn 3:16-21
Whit-Tuesday	Act 8:14-17	Jn 10:1-10
Trinity Sunday	Rom 11:33-36	Mt 28:18-20
Corpus Christi	1 Cor 11:23-29	Jn 6:56-59
After Pentecost, 2	1 Jn 3:13-18	Lk 14:16-24
Sacred Heart	Eph 3:8-19	Jn 19:31-37
After Pentecost, 3	1 Pt 5:6-11	Lk 15:1-10
After Pentecost, 4	Rom 8:18-23	Lk 5:1-11
After Pentecost, 5	1 Pt 3:8-15	Mt 5:20-24
After Pentecost, 6	Rom 6:3-11	Mk 8:1-9
After Pentecost, 7	Rom 6:19-23	Mt 7:15-21
After Pentecost, 8	Rom 8:12-17	Lk 16:1-9
After Pentecost, 9	1 Cor 10:6-13	Lk 19:41-47
After Pentecost, 10	1 Cor 12:2-11	Lk 18:9-14
After Pentecost, 11	1 Cor 15:1-10	Mk 7:31-37
After Pentecost, 12	2 Cor 3:4-9	Lk 10:23-37
After Pentecost, 13	Gal 3:16-22	Lk 17:11-19
After Pentecost, 14	Gal 5:16-24	Mt 6:24-33
After Pentecost, 15	Gal 5:25;6:1-10	Lk 7:11-16
After Pentecost, 16	Eph 3:13-21	Lk 14:1-11
After Pentecost, 17	Eph 4:1-16	Mt 22:35-46
After Pentecost, 18	1 Cor 1:4-8	Mt 9:1-8
After Pentecost, 19	Eph 4:23-28	Mt 22:1-14
After Pentecost, 20	Eph 5:15-21	Jn 4:46-53
After Pentecost, 21	Eph 6:10-17	Mt 18:23-35
After Pentecost, 22	Phil 1:6-11	Mt 22:15-21

| After Pentecost, 23 | Phil 3:17;4:3 | Mt 9:18-26 |
| After Pentecost, 24 | Col 1:9-14 | Mt 24:15-35 |

FEASTS OF THE SAINTS

St. Andrew, Nov. 30	Rom 10:10-18	Mt 4:18-22
Immaculate Conception, Dec. 8	Prv 8:22-35	Lk 1:26-28
St. Thomas, Dec. 21	Eph 2:19-22	Jn 20:24-29
Conversion of St. Paul, Jan. 25	Act 9:1-22	Mt 19:27-29
Candlemas, Feb. 2	Mal 3:1-4	Lk 2:22-32
St. Matthias, Feb. 24	Act 1:15-26	Mt 11:25-30
St. Patrick, March 17	Sir 44:16-27;45:3-20	Mt 25:14-23
St. Joseph, March 19	Sir 45:1-6	Mt 1:18-21
Annunciation, March 25	Is 7:10-15	Lk 1:26-38
St. George, April 23	2 Ti 2:8-10;3:10-12	Jn 15:1-7
St. Mark, April 25	Ez 1:10-14	Lk 10:1-9
Sts. Philip and James, May 11	Wis 5:1-5	Jn 14:1-13
St. Barnabas, June 11	Act 11:21-26; 13:1-3	Mt 10:16-22
St. John Baptist, June 24	Is 49: 1-8	Lk 1:57-68
Sts. Peter, Paul, June 29	Act 12:1-11	Mt 16:13-19
Visitation B.V.M., July 2	Ct 2:8-14	Lk 1:39-47
St. Mary Mag., July 22	Ct 3:2-5;8:6-7	Lk 7:36-50
St. James, July 25	1 Cor 4:9-15	Mt 20:20-23
St. Ann, July 26	Prv 31:10-31	Mt 13:44-52
Transfiguration, Aug. 6	2 Pt 1:16-19	Mt 17:1-9
St. Lawrence, Aug. 10	2 Cor 9:6-10	Jn 12:24-26
Assumption, August 15	Sir 24:11-20	Lk 1:41-50
St. Bartholomew, Aug.24	1 Cor 12:27-31	Lk 6:12-19
Nativity B.V.M., Sep. 8	Prv 8:22-35	Mt 1:1-16
St. Matthew, Sep. 21	Ez 1:10-14	Mt 9:9-13
St. Michael, Sep. 29	Ap 1:1-5	Mt 18:1-10
Guardian Angels, Oct. 2	Ex 23:20-23	Mt 18:1-10
St. Luke, Oct. 18	2 Cor 8:16-24	Lk 10:1-9
Sts. Simon and Jude, Oct. 28	Eph 4:7-13	Jn 15:17-25
All Saints, Nov. 1	Ap 7:2-12	Mt 5:1-12
All Souls, Nov. 2	1 Cor 15:51-57	Jn 5:25-29
Presentation B. V. M., Nov. 21	Sir 24:14-16	Lk 11:27-28

APPENDIX X

DOCTRINAL INDEX OF SCRIPTURE TEXTS

Of necessity, only the more important doctrines of the Church are considered here and only some of the texts are given for these doctrines. This index has been inserted into this book for apologetical purposes. If we can demonstrate to our non-Catholic brethren the fact that our doctrines may be found in Scripture as well as Tradition, we may more readily be able to convince them of the truth of our claims. The preacher and teacher may also find this index useful.

ADAM
    Gn 1:26-27; 2:7-8; 3:1-24;
    5:4-5
ANGELS
    Bad
    2 Pt 2:4
    Jude 1:6
    Guardian
    Tb 12:12,15
    Mt 18:10
    Heavenly Messengers
    Lk 1:26-28
ASCENSION OF CHRIST
    Mk 16:19-20
    Lk 24:50-51
    Act 1:9-11
ASHES (BLESSED)
    Jb 42:6

Jon 3:6
BAPTISM
    Mt 28:18-20
    Mk 1:6-8; 16:15-16
    Jn 3:5
    Act 2:38
    Rom 8:14-17
BAPTISM (NECESSARY FOR
    SALVATION)
    Mk 16:15-16
    Jn 3:5
BEATITUDES
    Mt 5:3-10
BIBLE IS INSPIRED
    Is 8:1
    Jer 30:2
    Ex 34:27
    Mt 22:43

2 Tm 3:15
2 Pt 3:15-16
BIRTH OF CHRIST (See Jesus Christ)
BLESSINGS
Gn 27:34
Dt 10:8
Mt 19:13-15
Mk 8:5-6
Lk 24:50
1 Cor 10:16
CATHOLIC CHURCH
Apostolicity of
Mt 16:18
Eph 2:19-20
Authority of
Mt 18:17
Lk 10:16
Act 20:28
2 Cor 5:20
Brings men to salvation
Jn 3:16-17; 20:19-23
Holiness of
Mt 7:15-20
Ti 2:13-14
1 Jn 3:5
Indefectibility of
Mt 16:18; 28:20
Infallibility of
Jn 14:16; 26
Necessity of
Mk 16:15-16
Lk 10:16
Oneness of
Mal 1:11
Jn 17:11, 17, 21
1 Cor 10:17
Eph 4:4-6
Universality of
Mt 24:14
Mk 16:15-16

Act 1:8
Rom 10:17-18
CELIBACY
Mt 19:11-12
1 Cor 7:38-40
CEREMONIES
Ex 12:24-27
Neh 13-14
Jn 9:6-7; 20:22
CHARITY
1 Cor 13:1-7; 13:13
Col 3:14
Eph 4:2
1 Pt 4:8
COMMANDMENTS
Ten
Ex 20:1-17
Mt 5:17-19
Two Greatest
Mt 22:35-40
COMMUNION
Jn 6:54-59
Act 2:42
See Eucharist
Under one kind
Lk 24:30
Jn 6:51,58
Act 2:42; 20:7
Of Saints
2 Mc 12:46
Eph 2:21-22
Col 1:12
Heb 12:22-24
CONFIRMATION
Jn 7:38-39; 16:7
Act 2:1-4; 8:14-16; 19:5-6
CONTRITION
Is 55:7
Ez 18:27-28
Lk 7:36-50; 15:17-24; 23:39-43

CREATION OF THE WORLD
  Gn 1:1,27
  Act 17:24-26
DEAD, PRAYING FOR
  2 Mc 12:46
DEATH OF JESUS
  Mt 27:45-50
  Mk 15:33-37
  Lk 23:44-49
  Jn 19:25-30
DESCENT OF CHRIST INTO
  HELL (LIMBO)
  Act 2:24
  1 Pt 3:19f; 4:6
DIVORCE (See Matrimony)
EUCHARIST
  Institution of
    Mt 26:26-28
    Mk 14:22-24
    Lk 22:19-20
    1 Cor 11:23-29
  Promise of
    Jn 6:48-59
EVE
  Gn 1:28; 2:18,21-25; 3:1-20;
    4:1
EXORCISM
  Mk 5:1-3; 16:17
  Lk 9:1; 10:17
EXTREME UNCTION
  Mk 6:12-13
  Jas 5:14-15
FAITH
  Mt 16:15-17
  Jn 3:31-33; 20:29
  1 Jn 5:9
  Heb 11:1-2
FASTING (AND ABSTAINING)
  Tb 12:8
  Jl 2:12
  Mt 4:1-2; 6:16-18

FATHER, GOD THE
  Jn 5:18
  2 Cor 1:3
GOD
  Attributes of
    Ex 3:14
    Lu 19:2
    Tb 3:2
    Is 44:6
    Ps 102:8; 138:7-10; 146-5
    Lk 1:37
    Heb 4:13
    Ap 1:18
  Existence known from reason
    Wis 13:1-9
    Rom 1:19-23
  Nature of
    Ex 3:14f
  One
    Is 45:5
GOOD WORKS
  Necessity of
    Mt 3:10
    Gal 6:6-10
    Jas 1:22; 2:26
    3 Jn 1:5
GRACE
  Actual
    Jn 15:5
    Eph 1:17-18
    Phil 2:13
  Sanctifying
    Jn 1:12; 14-23
    Rom 8:14-17
    1 Cor 6:19-20
    Gal 6:15
    Heb 12:28
    1 Jn 3:1
HEAVEN
  Mt 25:34
  Jn 17:3

NOTES

PART ONE

1. J. Steinmueller and K. Sullivan, *Catholic Biblical Encyclopedia, New Testament* (New York, N. Y., Joseph F. Wagner, Inc., 1950), 72.

2. J. Laux, *Introduction to the Bible* (New York, N. Y., Benziger Brothers, 1932), 18.

3. J. J. Dougherty, *Scripture Lectures*—ad usum privatum (Darlington, N. J., Immaculate Conception Seminary, 1943) I, 70.

4. A. Robert and A. Tricot, *Guide to the Bible* (Westminster, Md., Newman Press, 1951; now New York, Desclee & Co.) I, 16.

5. *Ibid.*

6. *Ibid.*, 19.

7. *Ibid.*, 21

8. *Ibid.*, 22-23.

9. *Ibid.*, 44.

10. Dougherty, op. cit., I, 13.

11. *Ibid.*, 24.

12. The Bruce Publishing Company, Milwaukee, published the New Testament (1954) translated from the original Greek into modern English by J. Kleist and J. Lilly.

13. H. Graham, *Where We Got the Bible* (St. Louis, Mo., Herder Book Co., 1948), 105.

14. *Ibid.*, 107.

PART TWO

1. E. Power, "The History of Israel" in *A Catholic Commentary on Holy Scripture* (London, New York, Thomas Nelson and Sons Ltd., 1951), 84.

2. The dates quoted in this chapter are taken from *A Guide to Old Testament History* by Daniel W. Martin, C.M. (St. Louis, Mo., Kenrick Seminary, 1951).

3. Father Felix, *Old Testament Pamphlet Series* (Ireland, Catholic Truth Society) I, 20.

4. Dougherty, op. cit., II, 63.

5. E. F. Sutcliffe, "The Chronology of the Old Testament" in *A Catholic Commentary on Holy Scripture*, etc., 166.

6. Felix, op. cit., I, 9.

7. P. Heinisch, *History of the Old Testament* (Collegeville, Minn., Liturgical Press, 1952), 18.

8. E. F. Sutcliffe, "Genesis" in *A Catholic Commentary on Holy Scripture,* etc., 184.
9. *Ibid.*
10. Dougherty, op. cit., 36.
11. Heinisch, op. cit., 20-21.
12. Dougherty, op. cit., II, 69.
13. Sutcliffe, op. cit., 196.
14. *Ibid.*
15. Heinisch, op. cit., 79.
16. Dougherty, op. cit., 106.
17. R. Bandas, *Biblical Questions* (Huntington, Ind., Our Sunday Visitor Press, 1947, pamphlet), IV, 43.
18. E. Power, "Exodus" in *A Catholic Commentary on Holy Scripture,* etc., 215.
19. *Ibid.,* 216.
20. *The Holy Bible,* Confraternity of Christian Doctrine Edition, Vol. I, *Genesis to Ruth* (Paterson, N. J., St. Anthony Guild Press, 1952), 514.
21. *Ibid.,* 520.
22. *Ibid.,* 526.
23. E. Power, "Josue" in *A Catholic Commentary on Holy Scripture,* etc., 283.
24. Dougherty, op. cit., 128.
25. M. Leahy, "Judith" in *A Catholic Commentary on Holy Scripture,* 404.
26. T. E. Bird, "The Psalms" in *A Catholic Commentary on Holy Scripture,* 444.
27. M. Leahy, "Ecclesiastes" in *A Catholic Commentary on Holy Scripture,* 489.
28. P. P. Saydon, "The Canticle of Canticles" in *A Catholic Commentary on Holy Scripture,* 496.
29. Bandas, op. cit., I, 86.
30. *Ibid.,* 87.
31. Robert and Tricot, op. cit., 135.
32. *Ibid.,* 148.
33. *Ibid.,* 157.
34. E. F. Sutcliffe, "Jonas" in *A Catholic Commentary on Holy Scripture,* 670.

PART THREE

1. J. L. McKenzie, "Jewish World in N. T. Times" in *A Catholic Commentary on Holy Scripture,* 734.
2. *Ibid.,* 730.
3. J. Chapman, *The Four Gospels* (New York, N. Y., Sheed and Ward, 1944), 6.
4. *A Commentary on the New Testament* (New York, N. Y., William Sadlier, Inc., 1942), 292.
5. Steinmueller-Sullivan, op. cit., 7.
6. *Commentary on the New Testament,* op. cit., 239.
7. G. Ricciotti, *The Life of Christ* (Milwaukee, The Bruce Publishing Co., 1950), 246.
8. S. Hartdegen, *A Chronological Harmony of the Gospels* (Paterson, N. J., St. Anthony Guild Press, 1942), 14.
9. Ricciotti, op. cit., 256.
10. A. Jones, "St. Matthew" in *A Catholic Commentary on Holy Scripture,* 857.
11. Ricciotti, op. cit., 265.

12. Hartdegen, op. cit., 18f.
13. Steinmuller-Sullivan, op. cit., 122f.
14. T. Corbishley, "The Chronology of N. T. Times" in *A Catholic Commentary on Holy Scripture*, 848.
15. *Ibid.*, 849.
16. Jones, op. cit., 859.
17. W. Leonard, "St. John" in *A Catholic Commentary on Holy Scripture*, 983.
18. W. Farrel, *Only Son* (New York, Sheed and Ward, 1953), 89.
19. Hartdegen, op. cit., 160.
20. Jones, op. cit., 902.
21. Hartdegen, op. cit., 189.
22. *Ibid.*, 190.
23. *Ibid.*, 192.
24. *Ibid.*, 192.
25. J. A. O'Flynn, "St. Mark" in *A Catholic Commentary on Holy Scripture*, 932.
26. H. Pope, *The Catholic Student's "Aids" to the Study of the Bible* (New York, N. Y., P. J. Kenedy & Sons, 1932), IV, 298.
27. C. Callan, *The Parables of Christ* (New York, N. Y., Joseph F. Wagner, Inc., 1946).
28. J. Kleist—J. Lilly, op. cit., 372-373.
29. Steinmueller-Sullivan, op. cit., 248.
30. *Ibid.*, 204.
31. *Ibid.*, 302-303.
32. Kleist-Lilly, op. cit., 650.
33. Dougherty, op. cit., III, 40.

BIBLIOGRAPHY

For some English Versions of the Bible consult text, p. 45.

THE BIBLE IN GENERAL

Dougherty, J., **Outlines of Bible Study** (Milwaukee, Bruce, 1934)

Graham, H., **Where We Got the Bible** (St. Louis, Herder, 1948)

Kinsel, P. and Henry, L., **Catholic Shrines of the Holy Land** (New York, Farrar, Straus and Young, 1951)

Lattey, C., **Back to the Bible** (London, Burns, Oates and Washbourn, 1944)

Laux, J., **Introduction to the Bible** (New York, Benziger, 1932)

Maredrous, Monks of, **Guide to the Bible** (London, Sands, 1953)

Orchard, B., General Editor, **A Catholic Commentary on Holy Scripture** (New York, London, Paris, Thomas Nelson & Sons, 1953)

Plassman, T., **The Book Called Holy** (Paterson, N. J., St. Anthony Guild Press, 1933)

Poelman, R., **How to Read the Bible** (New York, Kenedy, 1953)

Pope, H., **English Versions of the Bible** (St. Louis, Mo., Herder, 1952)

Robert A., and Tricot, A., **Guide to the Bible** (New York, Desclee & Co., 1951-55) 2 vols.

Rome and the Study of Scripture—Papal Documents; Decisions of the Biblical Commission (St. Meinrad, Indiana, Grail, 1953)

Rooney, G., **Preface to the Bible** (Milwaukee, Bruce, 1949)

Steinmueller, J., **A Companion to Scripture Studies** (New York, Wagner, 1948)

Steinmueller and Sullivan, **Catholic Biblical Encyclopedia—Old Testament** (New York, Wagner, 1956)

Thomson, N. and Stock, R., **Concordance to the Bible** (St. Louis, Mo., Herder, 1945)

Woods, R. L., **The Catholic Companion to the Bible** (New York, J. B. Lippincott Co., 1955)

THE OLD TESTAMENT

Bandas, R., **Biblical Questions**—Old Testament (Huntington, Ind., Our Sunday Visitor Press, 1943) 4 pamphlets

Bargellini, P., **David** (New York, Kenedy, 1954)

Boylan, P., **The Psalms** (Dublin, Gill, 1949) 2 vols.

Coppens, J., The Old Testament and the Critics (Paterson, N. J., St. Anthony Guild Press, 1944)

Felix, Old Testament Pamphlet Series (Ireland, Catholic Truth Society) 13 pamphlets

Heinisch, P., History of the Old Testament (Collegeville, Minn., Liturgical Press, 1952)

Heinisch, Heidt, Theology of the Old Testament (Collegeville, Minn., Liturgical Press, 1950)

Johnson, H. T., The Bible and Early Man (New York, McMullen, 1948)

Jones, A., Unless Some Man Show Me (New York, Sheed and Ward, 1951)

Kissane, E., Book of Psalms (Westminster, Md., Newman, 1954)

Martin, D., A Guide to Old Testament History (St. Louis, Mo., Kenrick Seminary, 1951)

McGrath, B., God's Herald—A Guide to the Prophets of Israel (New York, Wagner, 1954)

Monro, M., Thinking About Genesis (New York, Longmans, Green, 1953)

Moriarity, F., Foreward to the Old Testament Books (Weston, Mass., Weston College Press, 1954)

Ricciotti, G., History of Israel (Milwaukee, Bruce, 1955) 2 vols.

Steinmueller, J., Special Introduction to the Old Testament (New York, Wagner, 1942)

Van Zeller, H., Old Testament Stories (Westminster, Md., Newman, 1950)

THE NEW TESTAMENT

Bandas, R., Biblical Questions (Huntington, Ind., Our Sunday Visitor Press, 1943) 4 pamphlets

Bullough, S., The Church in the New Testament (Westminster, Md., Newman, 1950)

Bullough, S., St. Paul and the Apostolic Writings (Westminster, Md., Newman, 1950)

Callan, C., The Four Gospels with a Practical Critical Commentary for Priests and Students (New York, Wagner, 1940)

Callan, C., The Parables of Christ (New York, Wagner, 1946)

Catholic Biblical Association, Commentary on the New Testament (New York, Sadlier, 1942)

Chapman, J., The Four Gospels (New York, Sheed and Ward, 1944)

Green-Armytage, A., Portrait of Saint Luke (London, Burns & Oates, 1955)

Hartdegen, S., A Chronological Harmony of the Gospels (Paterson, St. Anthony Guild Press, 1942)

Holzner, J., Paul of Tarsus (St. Louis, Herder, 1944)

Knox, R., **A Commentary on the Gospels** (New York, Sheed & Ward, 1954)

Knox, R., **St. Paul's Gospel** (New York, Sheed & Ward, 1951)

Loenertz, R., **The Apocalypse of St. John** (New York, Sheed & Ward, 1948)

Maturin, B., **The Parables of Our Lord** (Baltimore, Carroll Press, 1951)

O'Brien, I., **Peter and Paul, Apostles** (Paterson, St. Anthony Guild)

Philipon, M., **The Mother of God** (Westminster, Md., Newman Press, 1953)

Prat, F., **The Theology of St. Paul** (Westminster, Newman Press, 2 vols.)

Retif, A., **John the Baptist, Missionary of Christ** (Westminster, Md., Newman Press, 1953)

Seraphin, E. & Kelly, J., **Maps of the Land of Christ** (Paterson, St. Anthony Guild Press, 1947)

Steinmueller, J., & Sullivan, K., **Catholic Biblical Encyclopedia—New Testament** (New York, J. F. Wagner, 1950)

Steinmueller, J., **Special Introduction to the New Testament** (New York, Wagner, 1943)

William, F., **Mary the Mother of Jesus** (St. Louis, Herder, 1941)

Zolli, E., **The Nazarene** (St. Louis, Herder, 1950)

JESUS CHRIST

Barbet, P., **A Doctor at Calvary** (New York, Kenedy, 1953)

Eaton, R., **The Man of Sorrows** (St. Louis, Herder, 1921)

Farrell, W., **Only Son** (New York, Sheed & Ward, 1953)

Felder, H., **Christ and the Critics** (London, Burns & Oates, 1924) 2 vols.

Fillion, L. **The Life of Christ** (St. Louis, Herder, 1946) 3 vols.

Goodier, A., **Passion and Death of Our Lord Jesus Christ** (New York, Kenedy, 1944)

Goodier, A., **Public Life of Our Lord Jesus Christ** (New York, Kenedy, 1944) 2 vols.

Graindmaison, L., **Jesus Christ** (New York, Sheed & Ward, 1930) 3 vols.

Lagrange, M., **The Gospel of Jesus Christ** (London, 1938-1939) 2 vols.

Lebreton, M., **The Life and Teaching of Jesus Christ Our Lord** (Milwaukee, Bruce, 1935)

Mauriac, F., **Life of Jesus** (New York, David McKay, Co., 1937)

O'Brien, I., **The Life of Christ** (Paterson, St. Anthony Guild, 1937)

Prat, F., **Jesus Christ** (Milwaukee, Bruce, 1950) 2 vols.

Ricciotti, G., **The Life of Christ** (Milwaukee, Bruce, 1944)

William, F., **The Life of Jesus Christ** (St. Louis, Herder, 1936)

Wuenschel, E., **Self-Portrait of Christ** (Esopus, N. Y., Holy Shroud Guild, 1954)

Pickl, J., **The Messias** (St. Louis, Herder, 1946)

THE BOOKS OF THE OLD AND NEW TESTAMENTS IN ALPHABETICAL ORDER

The abbreviations given for the books to the Bible are taken from the Confraternity edition of the Bible. These abbreviations have been used throughout this book.

THE OLD TESTAMENT BOOKS:

Abdias	(Abd)	Judith	(Jdt)
Aggeus	(Ag)	1 Kings (Samuel)	(1 Sm)
Amos	(Am)	2 Kings (Samuel	(2 Sm)
Baruch	(Bar)	3 Kings	(3Kgs)
Canticle of Canticles	(Ct)	4 Kings	(4Kgs)
Daniel	(Dn)	Lamentations	(Lam)
Deuteronomy	(Dt)	Leviticus	(Lv)
Ecclesiastes	(Eccl)	1 Machabees	(1Mc)
Ecclesiasticus—*Sirach*	(Sir)	2 Machabees	(2Mc)
1 Esdras	(Esd)	Malachias	(Mal)
2 Esdras—*Nehemias*	(Neh)	Micheas	(Mi)
Esther	(Est)	Nahum	(Na)
Exodus	(Ex)	Numbers	(Nm)
Ezechiel	(Ez)	Osee	(Os)
Genesis	(Gn)	1 Paralipomenon	(1 Par)
Habacuc	(Hb)	2 Paralipomenon	(2 Par)
Isaias	(Is)	Proverbs	(Prv)
Jeremias	(Jer)	Psalms	(Ps)
Job	(Jb)	Ruth	(Ru)
Joel	(Jl)	Sophonias	(So)
Jonas	(Jon)	Tobias	(Tb)
Josue	(Jos)	Wisdom	(Wis)
Judges	(Jgs)	Zacharias	(Za)

The New Testament Books:

Acts of the Apostles	(Act)	2 Corinthians	(2 Cor)
James, St., Epistle of	(Jas)	Ephesians	(Eph)
John, St.		Galatians	(Gal)
Apocalypse	(Ap)	Hebrews	(Heb)
1 Epistle	(1 Jn)	Philemon	(Phlm)
2 Epistle	(2 Jn)	Philippians	(Phil)
3 Epistle	(3 Jn)	Romans	(Rom)
Gospel	(Jn)	1 Thessalonians	(1 Thes)
Jude, St.	(Jude)	2 Thessalonians	(2 Thes)
Luke, St.	(Lk)	1 Timothy	(1 Tm)
Mark, St.	(Mk)	2 Timothy	(2 Tm)
Matthew, St.	(Mt)	Titus	(Ti)
Paul, St.		Peter, St.	
Colossians	(Col)	1 St. Peter	(1 Pt)
1 Corinthians	(1 Cor)	2 St. Peter	(2 Pt)

◊

INDULGENCES FOR READING THE BIBLE

An indulgence of three years is granted to the faithful who read the Books of the Bible for at least a quarter of an hour, with the reverence due to the Divine Word and as spiritual reading.

To the faithful who piously read at least some verses of the Gospel and in addition, while kissing the Gospel Book, devoutly recite one of the following invocations: "May our sins be blotted out through the words of the Gospel"—"May the reading of the Gospel be our salvation and protection"—"May Christ, the Son of God, teach us the words of the Holy Gospel":

an indulgence of 500 days is granted;

a plenary indulgence under the usual conditions is granted to those who for a whole month daily act in the way indicated above;

a plenary indulgence is granted at the hour of death to those who often during life have performed this pious exercise, provided they have confessed and received Communion, or at least having sorrow for their sins, they invoke the most holy name of Jesus with their lips, if possible, or at least in their hearts, and humbly accept death from the hand of God as the price of sin. *(Enchiridion Indulgentiarum, 694)*

PRAYER BEFORE READING THE HOLY BIBLE

COME, Holy Spirit, fill the hearts of Thy faithful and enkindle in them the fire of Thy love.

V. Send forth Thy Spirit and they shall be created.

R. And Thou shalt renew the face of the earth.

LET US PRAY

O God, Who didst instruct the hearts of the faithful by the light of the Holy Spirit, grant us by the same Spirit to have the right judgment in all things and ever to rejoice in His consolation, Through Christ our Lord. Amen.

(Indulgence of five years. Plenary indulgence, under the usual conditions, if the prayer has been recited daily for a month) ENCHIRIDION INDULGENTIARUM, 287.

PRAYER AFTER READING THE HOL BIBLE

LET me not, O Lord, be puffed up with worldly wisdom, which passes away, but grant me that love which never abates, that I may not choose to know anything among men but Jesus, and Him crucified.

I pray Thee, loving Jesus, that as Thou hast graciously given me to drink in with delight the words of Thy knowledge, so Thou wouldst mercifully grant me to attain one day to Thee, the Fountain of all Wisdom and to appear forever before Thy face. Amen.

(Prayer of St. Bede the Venerable)

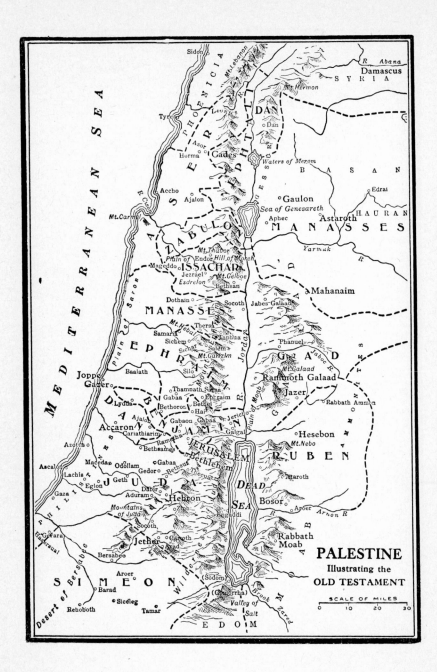

PALESTINE
Illustrating the
OLD TESTAMENT

SCALE OF MILES
0   10   20   30

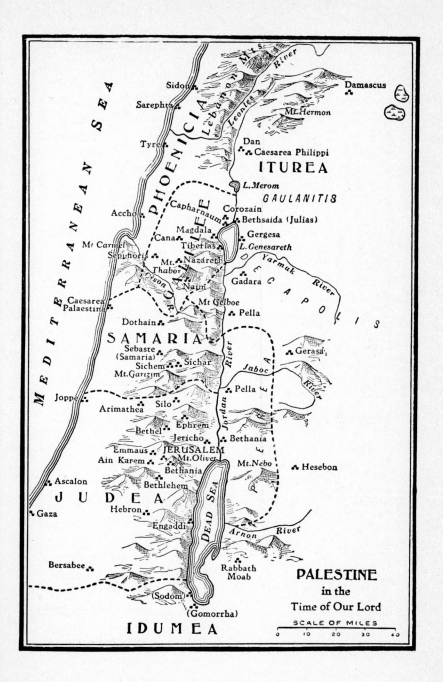

PALESTINE
in the
Time of Our Lord

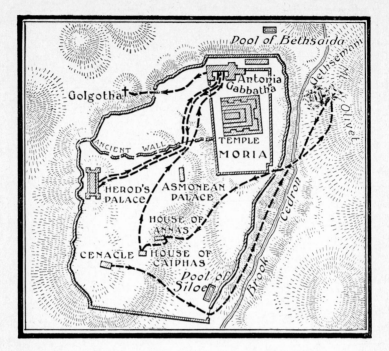

JERUSALEM, SHOWING CHRIST'S JOURNEY DURING HIS PASSION

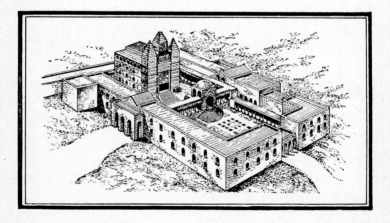

AS HEROD'S TEMPLE PROBABLY LOOKED

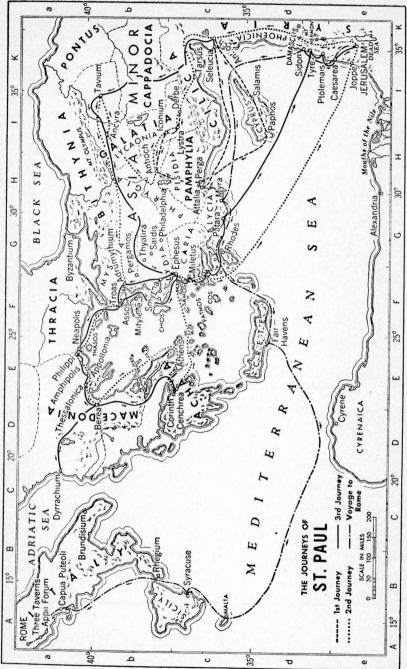

THE JOURNEYS OF
ST. PAUL

SCALE IN MILES
0 50 100 150 200

---- 1st Journey
······· 2nd Journey
—— 3rd Journey
-·-·- Voyage to Rome

Publications of the Society of St. Paul may be ordered from:

ST. PAUL BOOK CENTERS

2187 Victory Blvd.
Staten Island 14, N. Y.

St. Paul's Monastery
Canfield, Ohio

Old Lake Shore Road
Derby, N. Y.

138 rue Bowen Nord
Sherbrooke, Que., Canada

3442 McDougall
Detroit, Michigan

DAUGHTERS OF ST. PAUL

141 West Rayen Ave.
Youngstown, Ohio

78 Fort Place
Staten Island 1, N. Y.

325 Murray Street
Alexandria, La.

207 Broadway
San Antonio, Texas

196 Washington Street
Boston, Mass.

827 Fifth Avenue
San Diego, California